16/7/2010

AylesBury

DuBlin 24

40/10

ALEXANDER: KILLER OF MEN

ALEXANDER THE GREAT AND THE MACEDONIAN ART OF WAR

Other books by the author

The Nature of War in the Information Age

ALEXANDER: KILLER OF MEN

ALEXANDER THE GREAT AND THE MACEDONIAN ART OF WAR

David J. Lonsdale

CONSTABLE • LONDON

Constable & Robinson Ltd
3 The Lanchesters
162 Fulham Palace Road
London W6 9ER
www.constablerobinson.com

First published in the UK by Constable,
an imprint of Constable & Robinson Ltd 2004

A copy of the British Library Cataloguing in
Publication Data is available from the British Library

ISBN 1-84119-960-5

Printed and bound in the EU

For Mum and Dad

Contents

Maps

Preface

As a strategic analyst I am constantly aware that Strategic Studies is a practical subject. Or, as Williamson Murray and Mark Grimsley so succinctly put it, 'Strategy is the art of the possible.' Because of this, history remains the best teacher for those who study and/or practice the art of strategy. In my attempts to learn what is possible, I am constantly looking to the past for both positive and negative examples of strategy in action. It was this search that led me to Alexander the Great. In the field of strategic history Alexander stands out as potentially the greatest practitioner of the military art. His achievements, alongside those of men such as Napoleon and Hannibal, are revered. Yet, at the same time they seem too distant and too extra-ordinary to be of much use to us today. My aim in this book was to reconnect modern military strategy with the exploits of Alexander. Specifically, I wanted to understand exactly how he managed to be so successful, for so long, and against such a range of enemies. Through this analysis we can also further appreciate Alexander's role in the evolution of military practice. However, despite his achievements, it is important not to eulogise Alexander too much. Recognising that he had flaws as a military commander, and understanding what they were, is just as useful for the modern strategist as are his successes. Finally, I also wanted to convey the excitement of these remarkable campaigns to the reader. The history of Alexander's campaigns is one of an ambitious and courageous young man who conquered vast swathes of territory; and in the process elevated the art of war to an entirely new level. The title of this book, 'The Killer of Men', is a reference to the epithet given to the great Trojan warrior Hector, who was slain by Alexander's hero Achilles. This title also seems apt for Alexander. During the campaigns described in this book, the army of Alexander was capable of killing large numbers of their enemies. Why they were so proficient at this, and how effective it was in achieving Alexander's larger goals, are questions that will be addressed in this work.

My association with the subject of Alexander the Great has been a lengthy one. Therefore, inevitably many people along the way have contributed to this work. As always, I would like to thank Colin S. Gray, who remains a great inspiration to me. Thanks must also go to Malcolm Davis, Christopher Tuck and Stuart Griffin, who were always willing to discuss Alexander, no matter what the time or circumstance. Over the years I gained invaluable feedback and encouragement from my past students at the Joint Services Command and Staff College. Their enthusiasm for Alexander was a constant joy. I also greatly appreciate the support that I have received from my new colleagues and students in the Politics and International Relations Department at the University of Reading. My MA students in particular have probably learnt more about Alexander than they ever wanted to. As always, the support of my family has been invaluable and unstinting. Finally, I would like to thank my fiancée Maria Jose Moreira dos Santos, not only for her work to produce the maps that adorn this book, but also for her patience and unwavering love and support.

Chronology of Main Events

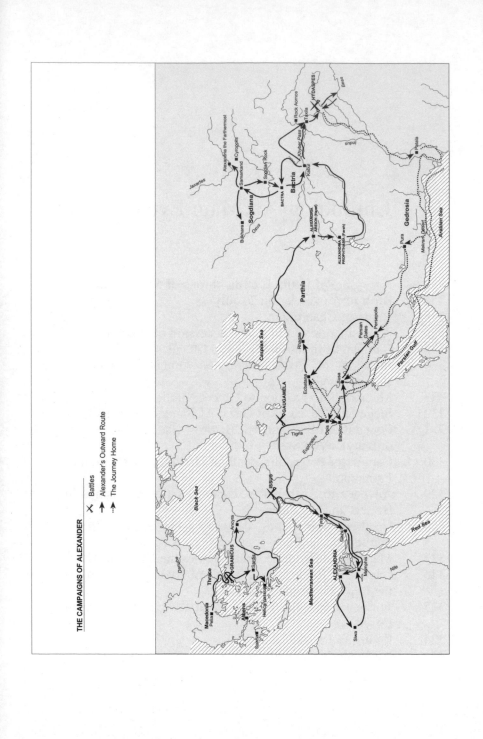

THE CAMPAIGNS OF ALEXANDER

X   Battles
↑   Alexander's Outward Route
··↑ The Journey Home

Introduction

The campaigns of Alexander the Great seem completely removed from our experiences in the modern world. The events that this book describes occurred over 2,300 years ago. Whether it is the great battle on the plain of Gaugamela, or Alexander's counter-insurgency campaign in Bactria and Sogdiana; these events involved people and places that seem alien to us now. And yet, at the time of writing Coalition forces are waging a campaign in modern Iraq, the site of the battle of Gaugamela, and forces from the same coalition are conducting counter-terrorism operations in and around modern Afghanistan, the area Alexander knew as Bactria and Sogdiana. The world may have left behind many of the things that were familiar to Alexander; but war has remained an ever-present feature of man's experience. Indeed, since war is synonymous with the passage of history, so the history books are replete with accounts of conflict. Within the historical literature on war a handful of military practitioners stand out from the rest. Figures such as Hannibal and Napoleon are credited with displaying an unusually harmonious combination of the qualities required to excel in the practice of military strategy. Even amongst these illustrious names, Alexander stands apart. Over a twelve-year period he enjoyed success against a range of different foes, often with forces superior in number to his own. Geographically, his campaigns stretched from the river Danube in Europe, through the Middle East and on into India. His foes ranged from the regular forces of the Persian Empire to a vast array of insurgents that his conquests provoked. Alexander successfully commanded forces in open plains, urban environments and dense, mountainous terrain. It is because he achieved such outstanding and continuous success across the spectrum of warfare, and in such an variety of terrains that he still commands such attention today.

Alexander has continued to inspire many books, television documentaries and films. Understandably, historians produce the majority of the work written on Alexander. Particularly noteworthy in this field are the works of Nicholas Hammond and A. B. Bosworth. These two authors have produced valuable general histories of Alexander's life and campaigns. Alongside these general works, our understanding of Alexander has been greatly enhanced by specific studies such as Donald W. Engels' *Alexander the Great and the Logistics of the Macedonian Army*. Alexander has also attracted the attention of military historians of Greek warfare. In this literature, Alexander has been assessed in relation to the evolution of warfare, particularly with regard to the demise of traditional hoplite battle. Victor Davis Hanson has taken this line of argument further and indicated that Alexander and his father, Philip II, are an essential early part of a process in the development of a western way of warfare. For Hanson, the proclivity for a decisive clash of armies and the total warfare of the twentieth century can be traced back to these ancient times. However, the campaigns of Alexander are not just the preserve of historians. They have also inspired discussion and analysis of management strategies in the world of business. Thus, it is clear that the literature on Alexander is plentiful and varied. However, despite such a broad coverage there is a curious scarcity of analysis from the perspective of modern military Strategic Studies. We are not completely devoid of military analysis however. In 1958 Major-General J.F.C. Fuller published what is still one of the most comprehensive and useful assessments of Alexander's military campaigns. However, since then the field of Strategic Studies has developed, and in particular has developed new concepts and analytical tools with which to gauge and understand the achievements of Alexander. It is hoped that, by utilizing a perspective grounded in modern Strategic Studies, this book will increase our understanding of Alexander's military prowess.

This work also seeks to avoid any moral judgements about Alexander's actions. Sadly, such judgements do appear in some of the historical works on this subject. This is unfortunate as too often the strategic rationale or brilliance of an action can be somewhat lost in moral condemnation. Strategic Studies seeks to present an amoral analysis of military affairs. By doing so, we can objectively assess actions and/or individuals that as moral beings may cause us concern. In the search to understand best practice in strategic affairs we can, and should, be able to disentangle moral judgements from strategic ones. For example, Nazi Germany was an abhorrent state that promoted and engaged in repugnant acts. Nonetheless, there is value in recognizing, and seeking to understand, the military prowess that on occasions those in the service of Nazi Germany displayed. Likewise, despite the personal and emotional feelings that modern international terrorism may provoke, an objective analysis of this phenomenon is vital in our efforts to understand and then defeat it. A modern moral observer of Alexander's campaigns will find plenty to condemn. The treatment of the citizens of Tyre and the brutal counter-insurgency campaigns in India, are but two examples of such actions. However, we should also be able to judge the strategic efficacy of such actions. The slaughter of a defeated enemy may provoke a sense of moral outrage; but it may also be strategically the most logical course of action. Surely in such instances we can accept the latter, without denying the former. This amoral approach does not inevitably result in the praising of acts of brutality as a matter of course. In fact, often acts of brutality can be heavily criticised from a strategic perspective.

Throughout this work a number of key military terms will be used. It is therefore important that these terms are explained before we embark on the analysis of Alexander's campaigns. Perhaps Alexander's greatest strength was that his prowess reached far beyond the battlefield. His extraordinary success can only be fully explained by recognizing that he was astute at all the levels of strategy. The highest level of strategy is *policy*. Policy is simply the overall objective that is sought. For Alexander, there were a number of policy objectives motivating his campaigns. There was a sense of personal aggrandizement and destiny in the pursuit of heroic acts; a quasi-religious motivation to unify the Greek and Persian worlds; a desire to rule all of Asia; and a quest for revenge on Persia for its earlier invasions of Greece. It is important to understand the policy objectives because it is these that should determine the methods used in the campaign. Clearly, Alexander had some far-reaching and grand policy objectives. This may help explain the levels of effort expended and the totality of the campaigns.

Once policy has been established the political leadership must then devise a *grand strategy* through which to pursue the objectives sought. Grand strategy encompasses all the instruments at the state's disposal: diplomatic; intelligence assets; military; and economic. The key challenge in grand strategy is choosing the right instrument, or the right balance of instruments, necessary to fulfil the policy requirements. This decision will be influenced by a wide array of factors, including the policy itself; available resources; the nature of potential enemies; and the geopolitical environment, to name just four. Although Alexander chose the military instrument as the primary method through which to pursue his policy objectives, his grand strategy was far from being one-dimensional. Relative to his enemies and the scale of the campaigns, Alexander had only limited military resources at his disposal. Thus, he had to cement his military conquests with a range of actions that fit within the other instruments of grand strategy. For example, his extensive programme of city building was critical in a number of ways. It helped generate economic prosperity, cultural exchanges and political stability, as well as providing his army with bases of operations. Yet, whilst recognizing that the other instruments of his grand strategy were crucial to the success of the campaigns, this book is primarily concerned with Alexander's military operations. In a sense, his military strategy is the first amongst equals. Without his military victories many of the other elements of his grand strategy could not be sustained. For example, it would be difficult for Alexander to gain the acquiescence of a local population for long whilst a Persian army was still known to be roaming the countryside. Alexander's gains in a region would in all likelihood be negated as soon as his forces left the area, because the Persian forces could move into the area and reestablish control. This was a constant problem for Hannibal in Italy during the Second Punic War, British forces in the American War of Independence, and for American forces in Vietnam. In such instances, military victory is required to set the foundation for broader grand strategic success.

So, the focus of this book is Alexander's military strategy. However, military strategy is not simply about winning victories on the battlefield. The military instrument must be used in such a way as to be compatible with the overall policy objectives. As the nineteenth-century Prussian military theorist Carl von Clausewitz so correctly observed: 'War is the continuation of policy by other means.' In this sense, *military strategy* refers to the use made of military force in the pursuit of policy objectives. The relationship between policy and the military is a complex one. Eliot Cohen best described this relationship as an unequal dialogue. It is not simply a case of the political leadership demanding whatever it desires from the military commanders. Instead, both the military and political leaderships must discuss what is required; and just as importantly, what is possible. This is why the dialogue aspect is so important. However, it lacks equity because the military instrument must ultimately serve the policy goals. This relationship is at its most complex in a modern democratic state. In such circumstances the political leadership will have little understanding of the military instrument and may be more concerned with the domestic political environment. Likewise, the military may have little understanding of the political world. For rulers like Alexander the situation was, on the surface, much more simple. Both the political and military leaderships were joined together in the individual of Alexander. However, this unification of the two roles did create its own dangers. Without an external dialogue assessing the strategic rationale of decisions, there is not such an effective check on the strategic efficacy of certain actions. Thus, as Alexander became more brutal and less nuanced in his use of force in India, there was an absence of a higher political authority to temper the actions of his military leadership. In contrast, the lack of a genuine dialogue creates the opportunity for a more rapid decision making cycle. There is also the potential for more decisive actions. Alexander could decide and then act without consultation or consideration for factors beyond his immediate strategic concerns. Whereas, a decision that results from a dialogue may become diluted by broader political concerns. It is within the context of military strategy that Alexander's more excessive use of force can be judged. On occasions, seemingly brutal acts may serve the broader policy objective by coercing or deterring current and future enemies. However, excessive use of force may simply serve to inflame resistance, and thereby undermine the broader grand strategy. Thus, military strategy must be in line with, and serve, grand strategy.

Once a military strategy has been decided, it must be put into practice. This is achieved at the lowest level by *tactics*. Tactics simply refers to actions on the battlefield in the face of the enemy. So, for example, tactics is concerned with how a phalanx is deployed, how it engages the enemy, and how it interacts with other units such as cavalry or the light infantry. In this sense, tactics is very much about the details of combat. Each battle or contact with the enemy represents a tactical event that occurs in a distinct time and place. Of course, ideally one aims to be successful in every tactical event. However, to have a successful overall military strategy a commander must link his tactical engagements together, so that they serve the broader purpose. This is where the *operational* level comes into play. The operational level links tactical engagements with the overall military strategy. Again, this is important to the study of Alexander because he excelled at both the tactical and operational levels. The operational level can be thought of in both conceptual and material terms. Conceptually it links tactical engagements together in the service of military strategy. Materially, we can think in terms of a geographic area of operations, within which the commander at the operational level moves his army from objective to objective. The operational level contains a whole range of factors essential to the success of a military campaign. Amongst the most important are logistics and lines of communication, movements of the enemy, and decisive points in the theatre of operations such as cities and key terrain features. One of Alexander's outstanding character- istics was that he successfully commanded the army at all of the levels of strategy.

As noted, Alexander's achievements are also remarkable because he was able to operate successfully against a range of different foes. Warfare can take various forms. 'Regular' or 'conventional' warfare refers to conflict that occurs between similarly armed and organized forces. These forces tend to have recognizable formations and hierarchical command structures. They also tend to be greater in number then irregular forces, and in this sense they often gain a relative advantage from a concentration of forces in open combat. They are usually uniformed in some sense, and therefore are identifiable from non-combatants. Indeed, under the modern laws of war, military forces are required to distinguish themselves from civilians. Whilst the wearing of a uniform makes someone a clearer target for the enemy, this practice does afford them protection under the Geneva Conventions, for example if they are taken prisoner. In contrast, 'irregular' or 'unconventional' forces are often substantially smaller in number; may have no hierarchical command structure as such; often do not wear uniforms, indeed they often deliberately hide within the civilian population; and tend to favour operations that do not involve a concentration of force, instead preferring the tactics of hit- and-run and/or terrorism. Due to their lack of numbers and/or capabilities, irregular forces tend to rely heavily upon utilizing the terrain to their advantage. This may involve urban operations or, as in the case of the irregular foes Alexander faced, it may involve fighting in mountains or densely forested areas. Alexander was able to adapt his forces and command style to operate effectively against both regular and irregular opponents. Discovering how he did this, and why he was so successful, is the objective of this book.

In order to explain Alexander's extraordinary success this book is divided into six chapters. The first of these examines the development of Greek warfare. The chapter begins with an analysis of Greek warfare before the rise of Macedonia. In essence, this is therefore an analysis of hoplite warfare; a style of conflict that dominated Greece until the fifth-century BC. From here, the book will explain how the art of warfare developed from this quasi-ritualistic form to the more total and effective approach developed by Alexander and his father. It will be shown that these two Macedonian rulers did not produce an independent leap forward; rather they built upon developments already underway in the wider Greek world. However, the end result was an army much more effective as an instrument of strategy. Before we can effectively analyse Alexander's prowess as a commander, we must understand the military instrument at his disposal. Thus, the chapter then proceeds with a detailed description of the Macedonian army that Alexander would lead into the Persian Empire. Finally, there is an analysis of the battle of Chaeronea, in which both the army and Alexander were tested against their Greek neighbours. This first chapter outlines and utilizes the modern Strategic Studies theory of the Revolution in Military Affairs (RMA) to help us understand the various developments that took place in Alexander's art of war.

Having outlined the instrument at Alexander's disposal, the book then proceeds for the next four chapters to analyse this instrument and its commander in action. These four chapters take us from operations along the river Danube to the brutal campaign in India. Each of the four chapters deals with one of Alexander's major battles and some of the smaller scale engagements. Both have a vital role in helping us to understand the genius of Alexander. It is one thing to be successful in open battle against a regular opponent who deploys his forces in a fairly predictable fashion. However, to be able to adapt one's forces and style of command to protracted irregular warfare in unfavourable terrain against an elusive foe is the sign of military genius. Although each chapter deals with distinct battles and campaigns, the general flow of events will also be covered. This is vital in order to understand how the different engagements fit into the overall campaign. Chapter two covers Alexander's first tests as commander-in-chief in the Balkans campaign, and his short campaign to maintain his hegemony in Greece. Then comes Alexander's first great clash with the forces of the Persian Empire at the river Granicus. Chapter three deals with the second great battle of the invasion and Alexander's first face-to-face engagement with the Persian ruler, Darius III. Prior to the battle of Issus there are some interesting operational level manoeuvres, during which Darius out-manoeuvres Alexander. This part of the campaign also gives us the opportunity to analyse one of Alexander's most infamous sieges, at the island city of Tyre. This is a fascinating event in the campaigns. Tactically, the siege of Tyre is a great example of the proficiency and ingenuity of Macedonian siegecraft. However, from an operational and strategic perspective some questions have been raised about the sense in undertaking the siege in the first place.

The fourth chapter briefly describes Alexander's advance into Egypt, including another difficult and brutal siege at Gaza. From here, the chapter shifts its attention to the final showdown between Alexander and Darius at Gaugamela. However, in many respects this battle is not simply a rerun of the battle of Issus. At Issus the battle was fought on ground favourable to Alexander, whereas the battle of Gaugamela was conducted on ground not only chosen by Darius, but also prepared exactly to suit the Persian forces. In addition, at Gaugamela Alexander was vastly outnumbered. With these conditions in mind, it is fascinating to analyse how the young Macedonian king was able to achieve such a decisive victory in this final engagement with the Persian ruler. The post-Gaugamela period presents Alexander with two interesting military challenges. The first, against the Uxians, reveals Alexander's ruthless ability to deceive his opponents and his ability to conjure-up favourable circumstances prior to battle. The second challenge was faced on the march to capture the Persian capital of Persepolis. Facing substantial enemy forces in an easily defendable pass, Alexander's outflanking manoeuvre is truly outstanding.

The final chapter dealing with the great battles shifts the geographic focus to Afghanistan and India. Before Alexander can fulfil his desire to invade India, he has to spend two years quelling a determined insurgency in

Bactria and Sogdiana. Chapter five focuses on some of the main events in this counter-insurgency campaign to illustrate the problems faced by Alexander, and the innovative and less-innovative ways in which he overcame them. This campaign also provides us with some of Alexander's most daring and astonishing actions, including the capture of seemingly impregnable fortresses atop steep mountains. India provides the setting for Alexander's last great set-piece battle at the river Hydaspes. This engagement provides us with an outstanding example of how to overcome the problem of making an opposed river crossing. The chapter concludes by briefly describing the final stages of the campaigns and Alexander's march back to the heart of his new empire, where he died at the age of thirty-two.

The four chapters outlined above cover twelve years of campaigning against a wide range of enemies, and in a vast array of different geographic settings. The concluding chapter will explain how Alexander was able to be so continuously successful for such a long period of time in such circumstances. In order to do this, the chapter will analyse Alexander's campaigns from a number of perspectives. These are: the army; the command style; Alexander's tactical, operational and strategic performance; and the quality of his enemies. Finally, the chapter will conclude by asking just how revolutionary Alexander's style of warfare was, and what general lessons can be drawn from these remarkable events that occurred nearly 2,500 years ago.

1

The Development of Greek Warfare

In order to understand the significance of Alexander's developments in warfare, we must begin by outlining what came before him. It is only after describing earlier Greek warfare that we can comprehend exactly how Alexander, and his father Philip II, achieved such decisive victories. Prior to the rise of Macedonia, Greek warfare had been largely dominated by the hoplite phalanx. This heavy infantry formation had been the tactic of choice for the Greek city-states, and had proven remarkably successful against Persian forces as well. Before the arrival of Philip and Alexander, the upheaval within Greece that came with the Peloponnesian War (431–04 BC) had already begun to erode the dominance of the hoplite. In this sense, Greek warfare was already undergoing some significant developments in the fifth and fourth centuries. Nonetheless, it took Philip and Alexander to bring many of these developments together in a coherent and mature fashion. However, Alexander and his father did not just take what was already there and weld them together more effectively; they

15

introduced a number of key innovations themselves. A key question then is: did Macedonia revolutionize the art of warfare, or were these developments merely the maturation of an evolutionary process? The defence profession provides us with a useful tool to help answer this question. In recent years the modern defence community has been dominated by the so-called 'Revolution in Military Affairs' (RMAs). Put simply, an RMA occurs when certain developments in warfare are exploited in such a way that massive military advantage is gained over those employing the older forms of warfare. In this chapter we will utilize the RMA concept in order to understand just how revolutionary Alexander's style of warfare was. By doing this, we can then begin to better understand why Alexander was so decisively successful on the battlefield.

Revolutions in Military Affairs

A number of RMAs have been identified throughout history. Four of the more obvious RMAs are the gunpowder, Napoleonic, airpower and nuclear revolutions. What constitutes an RMA? RMAs can have a number of origins. New technological developments are frequently at the forefront of any substantial change. Often just as important as the technological dimension is the political factor. Changes in the socio-political order can help unleash or guide the development of an RMA. It may be the case that certain advances in the art of warfare can only be pursued in the aftermath of significant changes in the political environment. Equally, certain political objectives

16

may dictate the direction that change takes. However, new technology and political conditions alone are not sufficient to induce significant relative advantage in warfare. Any new, or maturing piece of technology must be integrated and used effectively. This often requires new tactical and operational concepts. In turn, for these new concepts to be fully realized an armed force must be reorganised into new organisational structures.

A classic example that most clearly reveals how an RMA can occur is the development of Blitzkrieg during the twentieth century. In this particular case, a range of new technologies had appeared that could be utilized to enhance the art of warfare. The internal combustion engine made possible the development of the tank and its supporting logistics and infantry vehicles. Together, these vehicles enabled more rapid manoeuvres in the theatre of operations. When a force rapidly increases its pace of advance there is always the potential that the entire operation becomes disjointed and chaotic. In this sense, the advent of wireless radio was an adequate solution to this problem. Taken together, these two technological developments produced forces that could move rapidly in a coordinated manner, and thereby achieve a higher tempo of operations.

However, as noted above, merely having the technological capability is not enough. A doctrine, or operating procedures if you will, was required to get the most out of this combination of technologies. It is interesting to note that the various European armies utilized their new forces differently in the early stages of the Second World War. These differences can be largely explained by the different political and strategic circumstances of the countries. The

French, who had a defensive and conservative outlook, spread their tanks throughout their existing infantry formations, essentially treating them as mobile artillery. In this sense, the French were certainly not doing anything revolutionary with their new technological acquisitions. In contrast, Nazi Germany developed the operational concept of Blitzkrieg. Within this new doctrine the armoured forces were concentrated, and acted as the spearhead of rapid offensive formations. This doctrine reflected the revolutionary and revisionist nature of Nazism, and also suited the strategic requirements of Germany at that time. As in the First World War, Germany potentially faced a war on two fronts against enemies with substantial resources at their disposal. This geostrategic reality translated into the need for forces that could rapidly defeat one enemy, before turning to face the other. Here is a clear example of political circumstances driving the development of an RMA. However, the doctrine of Blitzkrieg was not entirely new. Towards the end of the First World War both sides had developed operational concepts that formed the foundation for Blitzkrieg. In their attempts to break the deadlock of the trenches, both sides had developed self-contained formations that conducted deep and rapid advances along a narrow axis of attack. The architects of Blitzkrieg, men such as Heinz Guderian, further developed these ideas with the aid of the maturing technologies.

One of the greatest dangers for units with the task of rapidly advancing deep into the enemy's rear is that they may become cut-off from the rest of the army. This is a particular worry for the lead armoured units in Blitzkrieg. Tanks are powerful instruments that can advance rapidly and deliver significant levels of firepower. Nevertheless, when operating on their own they are vulnerable to infantry armed with effective anti-tank weapons. With these concerns in mind, the Germans developed the Panzer division. This new formation contained tanks, infantry, artillery, and support troops. This range of capabilities gave the Panzer division a degree of self-sustainability, and meant that the different elements could offer each other mutual support and protection.

So, we can see from this description of Blitzkrieg how the different developments coalesce into the basic elements of an RMA. But, a question still remains over the relative effectiveness of this development in the art of warfare. Did Blitzkrieg give the Germans a distinct military edge? In the short term the answer is a resounding yes. Blitzkrieg did indeed confer substantial advantages on the Germans in their invasions of Poland in 1939, France in 1940 and the Soviet Union in 1941. The forces facing the Germans could not initially cope with these rapid coordinated attacks deep into their territories. However, history clearly shows that the Germans began to reap diminishing returns from their Blitzkrieg operations. Germany was unable to maintain the levels of success they had achieved in the first three years of the war. This can be attributed to a number of factors, and is very significant in our analysis of RMAs. The weather and geographic depth of the Soviet Union neutralized many of the advantages conferred by Blitzkrieg. The Germans simply could not sustain rapid operational tempo in such conditions. Also, the substantial resources of their enemies meant that Germany could not translate their overwhelming tactical and operational successes into a

19

war-winning outcome. No matter how many Soviet forces were neutralized and destroyed, there were always more available. Significantly, Germany's enemies also slowly adapted to Blitzkrieg, either imitating it themselves, or discovering ways to offset its advantages. The significance of this section is to show that developments that produce substantial military advantage can eventually be offset either by the enemy or the environment. Therefore, an RMA has to be adaptable in order to remain effective. In later chapters, we will see that one of Alexander's great qualities was his ability to adapt the instrument and concepts he had used so effectively in his earlier battles.

So, how useful is the concept of the RMA to the study of Alexander the Great? The concept of the RMA has come under some severe criticism. It is alleged that it may simply be a construct of academics rather than reflecting any historical or contemporary reality. Likewise, it has been alleged that it may in fact be a creation of the United States defence establishment in order to justify increased defence expenditure. The logic behind this criticism is that by identifying a new RMA (in recent years this has been the Information Age RMA) the US military can justify increased investment in new technology. Nonetheless, despite these and other criticisms, the RMA hypothesis does provide a useful analytical framework when analysing military innovation. If the purpose of this book is to explain Alexander's outstanding military success, then the RMA hypothesis provides us with a range of useful concepts and ideas from which to start our analysis.

Traditional Hoplite Warfare

If one thinks of Classical Greek warfare the image of the hoplite comes instantly to mind. The historical evidence suggests that this form of warfare appeared sometime in the seventh-century BC, and would dominate the Greek world until the Peloponnesian War. The hoplite was a heavily armoured infantryman who took his name from the round shield (Hoplon) he carried into battle. The hoplite reflected a distinct socio-political structure in Greece. This development in infantry was based upon a new class of landowning farmers who could afford to arm themselves and defend their land. The hoplite was protected by bronze plate armour. Typically, he would wear a Corinthian helmet. This cumbersome bronze helmet offered substantial protection against blows to the head, but at the same time denied its wearer much of his hearing and his peripheral vision. Similarly, the bronze breastplate would deflect the vast majority of attacks from a range of weapons, including arrows, swords and spear thrusts. Yet, like the helmet the breastplate was heavy, hot and cumbersome. The concave shield was typically just over 900 cm (3 ft) in diameter. Because it was so large, to keep the weight down the shield could not be particularly thick. Even so, the hoplon still weighed approximately 7.25–9 kg (16–20 lbs). It was primarily constructed of wood, with a bronze facia. The shield was carried with a handgrip and arm support, although in the push of battle the hoplite could fix his shoulder under the rim. This practice would give his arm something of a rest from carrying the weight of the shield, but more importantly would enable him to push his bodyweight in against the shield. Finally, the hoplite may also have worn bronze leg greaves to protect his shins. Thus, for the period in question the hoplite was a relatively well-protected protagonist. In terms of offensive armament, the hoplite's primary weapon was a spear approximately 2.1–2.75 m (7–9 ft) in length. The spear had both an iron spearhead and a butt-spike at the other extremity. This latter device is believed to have served a number of purposes. In the first instance, should the spear break during combat, the hoplite could simply turn his spear around and continue to thrust at his enemy with the butt-spike. Also, the butt-spike could be used to dispatch any fallen enemy underfoot. The spear was essentially used as a thrusting weapon, and not as a missile to be thrown. Although the hoplite relied primarily upon his spear for offensive attacks, he also carried a short sword should his spear be lost or irrevocably damaged.

All told, the hoplite marched into battle with approximately 22–31 kg (50–70 lbs) of equipment weighing him down. It should also be remembered that the majority of the battles would be fought during the spring or intense Greek summer. One can only imagine the discomfort of marching and fighting in such conditions whilst wearing heavy bronze armour, carrying the substantial hoplon and wielding an 2.4 m (8 ft) spear. So, why did the hoplites use such cumbersome equipment? The answer to this question is to be found in the fact that the culture of hoplite warfare was not particularly offensive in nature. This may have had something to do with the nature of the troops themselves. As landowners and farmers they were chiefly concerned with the defence or limited acquisition of farmland. Hoplite warfare was not designed for rapid and destructive offensives to capture vast swathes of enemy territory. These were not professional soldiers who campaigned all-year round. Hoplite warfare was a very limited affair. In fact, it is fair to say that hoplite warfare was quasi-ritualistic in nature. Typically, the belligerents would meet on an agreed open plain for a decisive and short clash of arms to decide the issue in question. Battles would last for a couple of hours and were limited to daylight. In no way was this total or irregular warfare in which surprise night attacks or ambushes had any part to play. Nor were the civilian populations of the belligerents perceived as being legitimate targets. Although for those in the front lines the experience of hoplite warfare could be horrific and bloody, casualties were fairly light. Most battles did not produce casualty figures above 10 per cent. This was partly because, aside from those forces killed in the initial rout on the battlefield, determined and sustained pursuit of a defeated enemy was rare, and indeed discouraged. As we will see later with the battles of Alexander, pursuit was the moment at which the greatest slaughter of the enemy could occur. Pursuit rarely happened in hoplite warfare for two main reasons. Firstly, as part of the ritualistic nature of this warfare it was often commonly agreed by the belligerents that pursuit would not take place. Once an enemy had been recognizably defeated on the battlefield, an agreement could be reached whereby the victor gained whatever spoils were on offer, and the vanquished were allowed to return home to their farms. This was warfare between similarly minded and motivated people. Secondly, the forces involved were not well suited to engage in a pursuit. Before the rise of Macedonia, cavalry was an underused arm of military forces in Greece. Aside from states such as Thessaly and Boeotia, cavalry had never been developed to a point where it could challenge the well-armoured hoplite on the battlefield. The rugged geography of southern Greece restricted cavalry operations and made them difficult and expensive forces to maintain. Thus, without an effective cavalry arm, the burdensome equipment of the hoplite made pursuit an unattractive and somewhat impractical undertaking.

With such forces and conventions as those described above, what were the tactics employed in hoplite battle? The phalanx was the formation of choice for hoplite warfare. This was a close order formation several ranks in depth. The hoplites would stand in densely packed lines with a spear in their right hand and the shield on their left arm. In such a formation the shields would overlap, thereby ideally presenting a solid front of protection. The main side effect of this was that the entire line would edge to the right as each man sought protection from his neighbour's shield. The phalanx was typically eight or more men in depth. However, due to the length of the spear, only the weapons of the first three ranks protruded into the killing zone. The key to success in such a formation was cohesion and discipline rather than individual acts of glory. Indeed, maintaining the line was the primary concern of the phalanx. A cohesive and solid phalanx was a formidable defensive formation. It presented an enemy with a solid line and mass of shields and spearheads. However, should any gaps appear, or should the enemy get behind the phalanx, then the vulnerable flanks and rear would be exposed. In most instances this could spell disaster for the phalanx. Because of their heavy armour and the nature of their tactics, the hoplite phalanx was not a particularly mobile formation that could rapidly turn to protect its flanks and rear.

It is important to point out that the fighting during this period in Greek history was almost exclusively a clash of similarly armed hoplite phalanxes. Again, due to a combination of convention and practicalities there was little role for cavalry or light infantry forces in this form of warfare. The clash of hoplites in face-to-face combat fitted with the heroic tradition of Greek legend. Indeed, it was regarded as a somewhat less-honourable and cowardly act for a hoplite to be slain by an archer or any other form of socially inferior missile-wielding combatant. There were also practical reasons for the dominance of the hoplite over light infantry troops. As noted above, the heavy armour of the hoplite was fairly resistant to missile attack. The raised spears of the hoplite phalanx magnified this resistance as they marched towards the enemy. The density of the spears could deflect a number of the missiles launched against the phalanx. Also, the limited range of missile weapons in this period meant that there was only a brief period of opportunity to attack the hoplites before they were upon their foes. In a classic open-pitched battle, light infantry forces could ill-afford to be caught in the open by well-armed hoplites. Cavalry forces faced similar practical obstacles on the hoplite field of battle. In an age before stirrups, mounted troops did not possess such a stable platform from which to fight. Therefore, if they were faced with a solid and disciplined phalanx they would be unable to drive home a lance with the required force without becoming unseated. This is assuming that both horse and rider would have the courage to charge headlong into an unbroken line of spears and shields. In most cases, if a phalanx could maintain its solid formation it would be largely invulnerable from a frontal cavalry charge.

So, during this period, battle between Greek city-states was largely an affair conducted by opposing hoplite phalanxes. The details of how such formations fought at the tactical level are somewhat confused in the original sources. What is not disputed is the fact that the phalanx ideally required a relatively flat plain upon which to operate. Any obstacles or significant undulations in the terrain could make it very difficult for the phalanx to maintain its cohesion. For similar reasons, the phalanx was not well suited to rapid changes of direction and manoeuvre on the battlefield. The phalanx was a powerful, but somewhat restricted formation that lacked any significant mobility. In this sense, battles between hoplite phalanxes were rarely won by cunning manoeuvre on the battlefield, in which one side would fall upon the enemy's decisive point. Instead, the phalanxes would normally meet head-on in a shock action. At first the phalanx would move at walking pace towards the enemy. Initially, the spear would be held at a slope, but prior to engagement with the enemy it would be lowered and held in an underarm fashion. The phalanx would sometimes advance at the double as it came within range of the enemy's missile forces. Of course, unless well disciplined and well trained, this increase in pace could well reduce the cohesion of the formation. However, as the two phalanxes closed with each other they would normally reduce their pace back to a walk. Indeed, there is some evidence that on occasions a

26

phalanx would stop entirely to regain its cohesion before the clash of arms.

It is at the point of contact that there exists some confusion over how the hoplites initially engaged one another. The confusion concerns whether the initial blows were delivered with the spear held in an underarm or overarm position. On balance, the classical historians tend to agree that those hoplites in the front rank would have switched to an overarm position in order to stab downwards at the face and neck of their opponents over the shield. This fits the recorded evidence of the injuries hoplites suffered, and also reflects images depicted on a number of contemporary vases. However, if this were the case, one has to ask the question: if combat involves stabbing down at an opponent, why advance with the spear in underarm fashion? It has been suggested that this may have been for the safety of those behind the butt-spike. The answer to this dilemma may be that the front rank used their spears in an overhand fashion to stab down at their opponents, whilst the next two or three ranks created the shock collision with spears held underarm.

As the two forces finally engaged each other, a number of spears may have broken on impact with the enemy's bronze armour. The front lines of the phalanxes were now engaged in what John Lazenby describes as 'slogging it out'. Those whose spears had broken may have opted to use the butt-spike, or indeed may have unsheathed their swords.

Victor Davis Hanson paints a grim picture for those in the front lines during this stage of the battle. He describes how bodies could be piled two or three high at the point of contact between the two sides. Penetration wounds to the face and groin were common as the hoplites sought out the unprotected parts of their enemy's anatomy. Alternatively, heavy impacts on the Corinthian helmet could cause fatal internal damage to the brain of its wearer. Thus, although in general terms hoplite battle was often a limited affair, for protagonists in the front lines it was a high intensity, total experience.

At this stage of the battle the objective was to kill the enemy in front, and so begin to create a gap in the opposition's line. As gaps appeared, the enemy would desperately attempt to fill them with men moving through from the rear ranks. Alternatively, these gaps could be further breached and thereby expose the vulnerable flanks of the enemy's front ranks in that vicinity. On occasions, a breach in the enemy's line could bring victory fairly quickly. On seeing a breach appear, men in other sections of the phalanx might perceive the end was near, and thus the entire formation could begin to crumble as they made a bid to escape the battle. However, if no decisive gaps were created the battle would move onto a stage of 'pushing and shoving'. By now, the two phalanxes would literally be toe-to-toe and shield-to-shield. The men in the rear ranks would put their shoulders under the rim of the hoplon and push those ahead into the enemy. The objective now was to force the enemy formation back and drive it from the field of battle. For those in the front ranks the situation must have been desperate. In some sense they still attempted to dispatch their opponents with their weapons. Alternatively, if it had become too congested they would try to wrestle their opponent to the ground with their bare hands. There is

28

evidence that on occasions some in the front ranks were crushed to death or asphyxiated were they stood, their bodies unable to fall because of the crush of men.

What factors made the difference between victory and defeat in this style of warfare? There was precious little opportunity for tactical ingenuity in this style of combat. This constraint was multiplied by the fact that hoplite generals served alongside their men in the front ranks. Whilst this enabled them to inspire those around them, it prevented them from 'managing' the battle once it had begun. Perhaps the most adept in the tactical realm were the Spartans. However, even these professional hoplites from a militaristic society could show little ingenuity within the tight constraints of hoplite battle. The main tactic employed by Sparta was to place its strongest forces on the right wing. Because hoplite phalanxes had a tendency to edge to the right anyway, by placing their best men in this position the Spartans could often break the enemy's left wing and roll-up the remainder of their forces. There is some evidence to suggest that over time the Spartans developed this tactic to the point at which they could detach a section of the phalanx to manoeuvre around the enemy's left flank. A relative advantage in numbers could in theory make a difference, especially if a battle was concluded in the 'pushing and shoving' stage. However, as is so often the case in other forms of warfare, the key factor contributing to success was morale. The willingness of the men to stand face-to-face with the enemy, and a belief in victory, were especially crucial in such a limited tactical environment. In more fluid forms of conflict, inspired generalship, tactical ingenuity and tactical proficiency could turn battles. War is always an activity in which moral and physical forces interact. However, it appears that in hoplite warfare morale could decide a battle very rapidly. Indeed, there were many occasions when one side would flee at the sight of the enemy. The Spartans often had this effect on their enemies. In fact, they realized how significant this was and enhanced its effect. Spartan hoplites would wear the same uniform red cloaks into battle, and would try to unsettle their opponents with a steady advance at walking pace. Although, this latter technique may have also been intended to maintain the cohesion of the formation.

The Battle of Marathon

Hoplite warfare not only dominated conflict between Greek city-states, it was also an effective instrument against invading Persian forces. Perhaps one of the greatest examples of this is the battle of Marathon in 490 BC. This battle gives us an illustration of how effective hoplite heavy infantry could be if used correctly. At the beginning of the fifth century, Greek cities on the western coast of Asia Minor rebelled against Persian rule. This so-called 'Ionian Revolt' was supported by both Athens and Eretria. For their part, the Athenians supplied twenty-five ships to the rebels, whilst Eretria sent five. The rebellion enjoyed initial success. In 498 the Greek forces captured and destroyed Sardis, the Persian regional capital. From here, the rebellion spread further throughout the Greek cities in the region and even infected the island of Cyprus. However, logistical problems and a lack of reinforcements from the Greek mainland meant that the rebellion began to lose its momentum. At the same time, the

Persian ruler Darius mobilized increasing numbers of men, and went on the offensive against the rebels. Slowly the rebel forces lost many of their gains, and with the Persian recapture of the city of Miletus in 494 the Ionian Revolt essentially came to an end. However, this was not the conclusion of the affair. Like so many empires throughout history, having faced a revolt on its periphery, the Persian Empire sought security by extending its borders, and hoped to conquer the Greek mainland. Also, Darius wished to enact revenge on Athens and Eretria for their support of the rebellion. After a limited and failed expeditionary operation in 492, Darius organized the main invasion for 490. Prior to the arrival of the Persian forces Darius had attempted to gain submission through coercive diplomacy. However, Athens rejected these overtures and the stage was set for a Persian invasion of the Greek homeland.

The Persian fleet gained control of the Aegean Sea and was thus able to put ashore the 25,000 strong invasion army. The campaign started well for the Persians with a successful operation against Eretria. After a week-long siege, the city was betrayed. Once the defences of Eretria had been breached the Persian forces all but destroyed it. With the first of their main objectives met, the Persians could turn their attention to Athens. The Persian forces now sought a harbourage on the northwest coast of Attica where they could land their forces for the march on Athens. Hippias, an exiled Athenian acting as a military advisor to the Persian forces, recommended the Bay of Marathon for the landing. Marathon was a small village some 38 km (23 miles) from Athens. Its bay offered an ideal spot for the army to disembark. The beach was large enough for the 600 ships of the

31

fleet, and just beyond this was an open, flat and fertile plain that would be ideal ground for the Persian cavalry.

The Persian army landed without opposition and began preparations for an attack on Athens. An early warning system based on the use of beacons alerted the Athenians to the impending attack. Once news of the invasion reached the city, messengers were dispatched to both Sparta and Plataea calling for military aid. The news from Sparta was not promising. Their reply stated that for religious reasons reinforcements would only be available in six to seven days. The Plataean response was more encouraging, but they could only send approximately 1,000 troops. The Athenians decided that they would not share the fate of the Eretrians, and so 10,000 Athenian hoplites headed north under the command of Miltiades and Callimachus to face the numerically superior Persian invaders. Their objective was to contain the Persians and prevent their march on Athens. When the Athenians arrived at Marathon they deployed in a defensive formation at the southern end of the plain so as to block the route to Athens. Their defensive position was fairly secure. Their left flank was guarded by Mount Agrieliki and the sea protected their right. To protect themselves from a frontal assault by the Persian cavalry they placed felled trees to their front. For four days the two armies, who were now just 5 km (3 miles) apart, faced each other without moving. Neither side wanted to take the chance of making the first move. For the Athenians to advance into an open plain against a force three times its size and strong in cavalry would be to court disaster. Likewise, the inferior and more lightly armed Persian infantry would struggle against the hoplites in their prepared defensive position. On balance this represented a

32

small tactical victory for the Athenian generals. By establishing a defensive position that protected their flanks, they had multiplied the inherent frontal defensive qualities of the hoplite phalanx. They had also managed to deter the numerically superior Persian forces. In this respect, the Athenians had already achieved part of their objective. By taking up such a strong defensive position on the route to Athens they had already contained the Persians, and thereby had bought their city a few extra days to prepare for an attack.

Finally, one of the two Persian commanders, Datis, made the first move. The Persians had to take action because the entire invasion campaign could have lost momentum had they remained inactive. The Persians also had to factor-in the possibility that Spartan forces would eventually advance on Marathon to reinforce the Athenians and Plataeans. Thus, overnight Datis loaded some of his forces, including the majority of the cavalry, back onto the ships. With the Athenian hoplites stuck at Marathon, Datis hoped to outflank them by sea and attack Athens directly via Phaleron Bay. Artaphernes, the second Persian commander, was left with a holding force to occupy the Greek hoplites at Marathon. At the operational level this was a high risk, high payout manoeuvre. Datis should be congratulated for thinking outside the box and for utilizing the operational flexibility inherent in his naval forces. However, dividing one's forces is often a risky undertaking; and so it would prove for Datis.

Of course, Datis' departure did not go unnoticed, and Athenian scouts reported this development to Miltiades at about 5:30 in the morning. Upon hearing this news, the Athenian general displayed a substantial degree of moral

33

courage and insight, and decided to take his one fleeting opportunity to defeat the enemy forces. It was estimated that Datis' passage to Phaleron would take approximately ten hours, with a further few hours to disembark his forces. Miltiades took the decision to engage the Persian forces still at Marathon, and then return to defend Athens against Datis. This was another high-risk plan. There were two main dangers for Miltiades to overcome. In the first instance, he was taking a risk by moving his forces away from their prepared defensive positions to face the Persian archers. However, this was not such a worry, because as we have seen, archers were relatively ineffective against well-disciplined hoplites. The greater danger lay in the fact that even if the battle went well for the Athenians, they could still lose the war if they failed to return to Athens in time to save the city from Datis. Miltiades needed to achieve victory on the plain at Marathon within three hours.

In order to achieve a rapid victory, Miltiades took a calculated risk with his battle formation. Reminiscent of Hannibal's great victory at Cannae in 216 BC, the plan was to deploy a weakened centre, whilst placing the real strength of the army on the wings. If all went to plan, the centre would fall back, drawing the Persians into a trap. As they surged forward to finish the Greek centre, the stronger Greek forces on the flanks would begin to encircle the hapless Persians in a double envelopment manoeuvre. Of course, the main danger with such a plan comes from the possibility that the centre is so weak that rather than fall back it simply collapses, leaving the flanks exposed. In order to achieve the desired effect, Miltiades showed tactical ingenuity to create a weaker centre. He simply

34

widened the gap between the men in the centre and reduced the ranks in the phalanx from eight to four. It has also been suggested that by this method of deployment the Greek line would match the length of the Persian line, and thereby guard against an outflanking manoeuvre. The Greek centre was held by Athenian hoplites under the command of Themistocles and Aristeides. The right wing, again Athenian, was commanded by Callimachus. To complete the formation, the Plataeans held the left flank.

Thankfully for Miltiades, the Persians deployed their troops as he had expected. The Persian centre was manned by their superior infantry forces, with their front protected by archers. Inferior conscript troops and the remaining light cavalry held the Persian flanks. It has been suggested that the Persian cavalry at Marathon was primarily composed of horse archers. At six in the morning a trumpet call signalled the start of the Athenian advance. In true hoplite fashion the Greeks started at a trot, before advancing at the double to cover the ground in which they were within range of the Persian archers. As the Athenians advanced on their enemy the Persian archers made little impact on the hoplites; thus as the two armies clashed, Miltiades' disposition was still intact. With the forces now in contact the battle went as planned for the Greeks. The Persian centre began to make headway against their Greek counterparts, but not enough to break the Athenian phalanx. Instead, the Greek centre gave way as planned, and drew the Persians into the trap. The inferior Persian flanks could not stand against the heavily armed and disciplined Greek hoplites, and they began to flee the battlefield. In their rush to escape the advancing enemy some of the Persian forces drowned in a marsh to their rear. With the enemy flanks in flight, the Athenians and Plataeans on both wings broke off the pursuit and closed in behind the Persian forces still advancing in the centre. By now the Persians were in complete disarray. They had ceased to resemble an organized military force. Instead, they desperately tried to make their way to the shore to escape in their ships. As the battle drew to a close, 6,400 Persian troops lay dead and 7 of their ships were lost. In contrast, the Greek casualties were incredibly light; only 192 were killed. Amongst the Greek dead was their commander Callimachus.

Critically for the fate of Athens, this decisive victory had been concluded before nine in the morning. The Athenian forces could now turn their attention to defending their city against Datis. The Athenian troops marched at such a pace that when Datis' forces arrived at their disembarkation point, the Athenian hoplites were already south of the city and had taken up strong defensive positions. Faced with an opposed landing and in command of depleted forces, Datis decided to abandon the assault on the city, and returned to Persia. Miltiades and his men had achieved a remarkable feat. They had taken full advantage of their enemy's decision to divide his forces, and used interior lines of communication to defeat one detachment and then deter the other from landing. The Greek victory can be attributed to a number of key factors. The Greek forces at Marathon were blessed with an outstanding commander. Miltiades had shown tactical insight in his original defensive deployment, and then displayed remarkable moral courage and tactical ingenuity to defeat the forces under Artaphernes. In addition, the Greek heavy infantry had proved how effective it could be against enemy forces superior in numbers but less well armed and disciplined. This point is particularly evident in the way that the hoplites retained their cohesion in the centre, despite the fact that they were left deliberately weaker in that sector of the battlefield. Finally, there was the remarkable forced march after the battle to defend Athens from Datis. As we will witness in the following chapters, such rapid operational level manoeuvres were often critical to Alexander's own success.

The Decline of the Hoplite Phalanx and the Rise of Macedonia

The dominance of the hoplite phalanx began to wane as a result of the more ambitious Persian invasions, beginning in 480, and the Peloponnesian War. With the coming of the fifth century the hoplite panoply became lighter, and more importantly light infantry forces became more significant. This evolution in Greek warfare is significant when we consider the basis from which Philip II and Alexander would build their RMA. In one sense, the victories over the Persians at Marathon and Plataea (in 479) cemented the dominance of Greek heavy infantry. However, in a more general sense the scale of the Persian wars placed a greater emphasis on the effectiveness of a variety of forces operating in a range of environments. For example, the poorer sections of society, who had been excluded from hoplite warfare, were now required to man the Athenian fleet. The socio-political dominance of the landowning farmers was eroding. The Peloponnesian War was even

37

more significant in the evolution away from classical hoplite warfare. The two main protagonists in this war, Athens and Sparta, were diametrically opposed in their strategic culture and strengths. Athens was primarily a maritime power, with her strength resting on her naval forces and imperial possessions. In contrast, Sparta's power lay in its land forces, and in particular in its professional hoplite army. The main strategic problem for these two belligerents was the inability to match the other in their own environment. Athens could not defeat the Spartan land forces, no more than Sparta could match Athens at sea. Consequently, the Peloponnesian War would not be won by a decisive clash of hoplite phalanxes. Both sides had to search for an alternative route to victory. In this manner, the demands of strategy induced significant tactical changes.

The Peloponnesian War unleashed a range of forces and resources not typically seen in conflicts between two Greek city-states. The war became a protracted and total affair. Gone were the limited, quasi-ritualistic clashes of the past. Battle reached beyond the open agricultural plains favoured by hoplites, and into more varied terrains which were better suited to other types of lighter forces. An example that reveals the limitations of hoplites in more varied environments is the Athenian invasion of Aetolia. Demosthenes led three hundred Athenian hoplites and allied infantry to attack the scattered villages and light forces of the Aetolians. Rather than facing their invaders in open battle, the Aetolians instead opted for a guerrilla campaign. They used hit-and-run tactics, leading the Athenians into rugged terrain and inflicting an attritional toll on the hoplites with missile weapons, ambushes, and fire. When the Athenians finally retreated they had lost 120 valuable hoplites and many more of their allied infantry. A further breakdown in the conventions of classic hoplite warfare can be attributed to rise of mercenary leaders such as Iphicrates. Men such as Iphicrates led lightly armed skirmishers called peltasts. These mercenaries, named after the small wicker/leather shield (*peltai*) they carried, were armed with javelins and specialized in harassment tactics. Rather than engage in open battle, they would conduct raids and hit-and-run attacks against their enemies' troops and resources. These different approaches to warfare were a world away from the quasi-ritualistic clash of hoplites on open ground.

This was the military environment into which the rising power of Macedonia would emerge. However, rather than merely accept the existing doctrines and conventions, Philip II combined them in such an effective manner that the art of warfare took a giant leap forward. In achieving this there were two precedents for Philip to follow. Fuller reminds us that Dionysius of Syracuse and Jason of Pherae (c. 380–70) were forerunners in many of the innovations that Macedonia perfected. Indeed, mirroring Philip's later plans, Jason had intended to unify the Greek world and wage a war of vengeance on Persia. If it were not for Jason's assassination, Greek history may have been very different. Nonetheless, it was Philip II who unified the Greek world under Macedonian hegemonic rule and began the invasion of Persia. Alexander would continue this war against the old enemy. And, having learnt at his father's side, he would take the new methods of warfare and develop them even further. Philip became King of

Macedonia in 359 BC. The kingdom he inherited was militarily weak and divided by dynastic conflict. Yet, through outstanding military reforms, battlefield victories and cunning diplomatic manoeuvres, Philip transformed Macedonia into the dominant hegemonic power in Greece. More than that, he created a military power that could inflict decisive victories on both Greek and Persian armies alike. Alexander would later prove that this new military was also capable of sustained and effective campaigning in a range of different environments and circumstances.

When considering Macedonian military reforms with reference to the criteria of an RMA, we will see that all of the main characteristics of an RMA are fulfilled. Prior to the rise of Macedonia Greek armies had been characterized by part-time hoplite farmers, sometimes with the addition of mercenaries. In contrast, Philip created an army that was both imbued with national fervour and manned by professional troops. At the centre of his army was a Macedonian core fired by the powerful political force of nationalism and personal loyalty to the monarch. And, because of the resources and mineral wealth of an expanding Macedonia, Philip was able to create an army that could operate and train all year round. The Macedonian army was not restricted to campaigning seasons. Since we live in an era when professional armed forces are far more common, the advantages of regular training and preparation for war seem all too obvious. However, the significance of these factors should not be underestimated, especially in the context of ancient times. Throughout history, some of the most outstanding military organisations have gained much of their relative advantage from regular training. To appreciate the significance of training we must seek to understand the nature of military forces and the activity of combat. Militaries are complex organizations that consist of individuals. Also, military forces spend the vast majority of their time not waging war. In most historical periods combat is the exception rather than the rule for an army. To further complicate matters, when combat does occur it is a chaotic, uncertain, exhausting, dangerous and highly stressful environment. The challenge for the commander is to get it right first time. Somehow, he has to create the conditions whereby his men will perform effectively both as individuals and as a unit. Whilst the conditions of battle can never be accurately replicated, regular and realistic training should enable one's forces to operate instinctively and in a more disciplined fashion. To this end, the successful Macedonian and Roman armies both trained on a regular basis. For Philip's men, this meant forced marches of up to 56 km (25 miles) and extensive drilling. As we will see later, the results of this could be impressive. Philip forged an army that could march great distances at surprising speeds, or perform battle-winning manoeuvres in the heat of combat.

So, Philip had the raw material for an RMA. Next, he would need to develop innovative doctrine, as well as the organizational structure necessary to enact the new oper-ations. Perhaps the most notable feature of Philip's army was its combined-arms character. This was a much more complex and versatile force that the traditional hoplite armies of the past. The Macedonian army still operated phalangites – infantry forces in phalanx formations – but these were complemented with cavalry and various types of light infantry. Much of the historical literature on the Macedonian army places a great deal of emphasis on the use of the heavy cavalry as the instrument of decision in battle. Whilst it is true that it was the cavalry that would penetrate the enemy's line, and thereby inflict the killing blow, it is simply inaccurate to describe one force as the instrument of decision in combined-arms operations. The instrument of decision was the army in its entirety, not just one section of it. The tactics of the Macedonian army will be described in more detail later when we discuss the various battles of Alexander and his father. For now, a brief description will given of how the army operated in general terms. The infantry phalanx no longer delivered the main offensive blow. Rather, the phalanx would initially pin a section of the enemy's line by its presence in the centre. This left the heavy cavalry with the role of creating gaps, or exploiting any that appeared in the enemy's front. The cavalry would then force open these gaps and attack the enemy in the flanks and rear. With the opposing line breached, the cavalry could roll-up the enemy forces onto the pikes of the advancing Macedonian phalanx. A significant danger when conducting such an operation was that the army could become split into different sections, which could then be defeated in detail. In theory, an elite unit called the hypaspists (shield-bearers) solved this problem. Amongst the historians there is some discussion over how heavily armed the hypaspists were. For example, W.W. Tarn claims that they were probably armed in the same fashion as the phalangites. However, the roles in which they were used suggest that the hypaspists were more mobile than the phalangites. Indeed, the hypaspists were mobile enough to act as a linking force between the cavalry and phalanx. As the cavalry advanced, the hypaspists would follow immediately behind them leading the rest of the infantry forward. Macedonian battle tactics were completed by the role fulfilled by the light infantry and other cavalry units. These forces were deployed to the front and on the flanks to protect the rest of the army. Thus, we can see how much more evolved were the tactics, composition and organization of the Macedonian army. Equally, it is evident that each section of the army had a crucial role to play.

Technologically, the army of Philip and Alexander was not so very different from those that had gone before. However, small differences reflected substantial changes in operational and tactical practice. Bosworth describes the new infantry phalangites as being a cross between hoplites and Peltasts. The most immediately visible changes in the equipment of the phalanx were the replacement of the spear and hoplon with the sarissa and a much smaller circular shield. At 4.8 m (16 ft) in length, the sarissa was substantially longer than the traditional thrusting spear of the hoplites. It was constructed from solid cornel wood, and had a small iron head that was better suited for piercing armour than the hoplite spear. It also retained the butt spike. Due to its length the sarissa had to be carried underarm with both hands. Of course, this meant that the shield could not be carried on the left arm as the hoplon was. Instead, the much smaller and lighter shield had a neck strap, and so it only really covered the left shoulder adequately. The armour of the Macedonian phalangites was also relatively light, consisting usually of a bronze helmet and perhaps only leather or linen cuirasses. The armour could be light because the sarissa, being longer than anything the enemy would present, offered protection through its length. In addition, the light infantry would provide a degree of protection from missile troops. From an offensive perspective, the sarissa produced substantial changes in the method of attack. The length of the sarissa meant that more ranks could project their iron spearheads into the killing zone. This could produce a 40 per cent increase in the amount of metal facing the enemy. However, in a sense the sarissa restricted offensive action as well. Obviously, a 4.8 m (16 ft) pike could not be held in an overarm position and thrust downwards at the enemy. Rather, the Macedonian phalanx advanced at a steady walking pace with the aim of forcing back the enemy with a cohesive hedge of spearheads. On its own, the Macedonian phalanx would have been a relatively slow-moving, inadequately armoured and vulnerable formation. However, as an integral part of a combined-arms army it was ideally suited to its task. And, as will be described in Chapter two in relation to the manoeuvres at Pelium, the well-armed and disciplined Macedonian phalanx could have substantial psychological effects on an enemy.

The Macedonian cavalry were also endowed with new weaponry. They were armed with a long spear (xyston), again made from strong cornel wood and with a butt-spike. In addition, they also carried a short sword. The xyston was used to stab at the enemy horse and rider. In contrast, Persian cavalry were usually armed with two smaller spears that were sometimes thrown as javelins. All of the Macedonian cavalry seem to have worn bronze Boeotian helmets, but only the 'heavy' cavalry units (Companion, Thessalian, Allied Greek) wore cuirasses and shoulder guards. The usual tactical deployment for the cavalry was the wedge formation. Such a formation allowed the cavalry to shift its axis of advance rapidly, and was therefore crucial when seeking and exploiting a gap in the enemy's line. The wedge was also ideally suited to penetrate a narrow breach in the enemy's front and widen it. In this sense, the wedge formation gave the cavalry mobility, flexibility and punching power. Alexander also had at his disposal the Prodromoi. These light cavalry units appear to have fulfilled two functions. Firstly, they operated as scouts for standard reconnaissance missions. However, in battle they could be equipped with the sarissa. With such a cumbersome weapon on horseback the Prodromoi could not operate in the wedge formation. Instead, they deployed in much more open form, and could be used in either an offensive or defensive role in line.

So, the army of Philip and Alexander did indeed operate with technologically advanced weaponry, and clearly evolved operational doctrine to gain relative battlefield advantage. They also had a new political motivation to help drive the development of an RMA. But, what of the fourth characteristic of the RMA? How was the army organized? A detailed study of the organization of the Macedonian army can be found in the work of Nick Sekunda. The core of the army was recruited from the kingdom of Macedonia itself. It is within these units that the fervour of nationalism was to be found. Therefore, as the following chapters will reveal, these dedicated Macedonian units were central to the success of the entire enterprise. In addition to these core units, Alexander had at his disposal fine troops drawn from vassal princedoms on Macedonia's borders. For example, the Agrianians and Illyrians fall into this category. The Thessalian army also came under the command of the king. Greek allied forces were supplied under the terms of the League of Corinth, which was under Macedonian hegemony. Finally, a number of mercenary forces from Greece and the Balkans marched with the army into Persia.

Of course, in such a monarchical system as that of Macedonia, the army was under the direct control of the king. However, great commanders such as Philip and Alexander understand the need to delegate the tactical functions and running of such a force. To this end, the king appointed seven Royal Bodyguards, who it seems acted as the army's senior staff officers. These men were drawn from a unit of 'Bodyguards', who aside from guarding the king's tent, also appear to have served as the general staff of the army. The exact status of the bodyguards is unclear, since on occasions they are mentioned as a fighting unit in some actions. Moving further down the hierarchy from the Royal Bodyguards, we come across the Strategoi (generals), who command individual units and on occasion, divisions. Finally, there is mention of the hegemones, who act as sub-divisional officers. All of the above were recruited from the Macedonian nobility. How this command system functioned on campaign will be discussed in detail in the conclusion of this book.

The basic unit of the cavalry was the ile (squadron). Each ile had 200 men and was commanded by an ilarch. It seems that the ilarch would have a trumpeter at his disposal to issue orders in battle. An ile was subdivided into four tetrarchiai of forty-nine men, each commanded by a tetrarch. The tetrarchiai was built upon the wedge forma-

46

tion, and thereby gave the cavalry ile its flexibility. Depending upon the circumstances, two, three or four ile would be joined to create a hipparchy (brigade). These were under the command of a hipparch. The cavalry was not a homogeneous organization. There were essentially six different forms of cavalry in Alexander's army. The most significant was the Companion cavalry. This heavy cavalry unit was commanded by Alexander himself, and was recruited from the Macedonian nobility. It contained eight ile. Alexander fought at the head of the Royal Squadron, which also happened to be double in strength (400). The other seven ile were of normal strength and each was recruited from a different region of the kingdom. In battle, the Companions, with the Royal Squadron at the front, fought on the right wing and were always the first into the enemy's line. Just as important a unit as the Companions was the Thessalian cavalry. This force of approximately 1,800 has been described as possibly the best cavalry in the entire army. In battle they were given the vital task of holding the left wing of the Macedonian line. It may have been the Companions that broke the enemy's front line, but this action would have been redundant if the left wing of the army had been outflanked. The vanguard unit of this force was the Pharsalian Ile. The final heavy cavalry unit was provided by the allied Greek states. There appears to have been two hipparchies present at Gaugamela, fielding approximately 1,200 men. In terms of light cavalry, the Prodromoi have already been mentioned. There were other similarly equipped Thracian cavalry units in the expeditionary force. Mercenary cavalry also supplemented these lighter forces. Again, there appears to have been two hipparchies of these mercenaries at Gaugamela.

Amongst the infantry, the smallest subunit was the dekas. This group of sixteen men represented one file of the phalanx. Thirty-two files produced the basic organizational unit of the infantry: the lochos (company) with 512 men. Each lochos was commanded by a lochagos, and two or three of them produced a taxis (battalion). Each taxis was recruited from a different district of Macedonia. The main infantry units in the phalanx were the Foot Companions. There were six taxis of Foot Companions, each consisting of three lochoi, and producing altogether 9,000 phalangites. Within this force, a taxis under the control of Coenus had elite status and had the position of honour on the right wing at both Issus and Gaugamela. As noted earlier, a crucial linking force between the phalanx and the Companion cavalry were the hypaspists. There were roughly 3,000 hypaspists divided into six lochoi. Nicanor, the son of Parmenion (Alexander's second in command), initially commanded this elite force. The vanguard lochos, called 'The Royal Hypaspists', were chosen on the basis of their height and had the place of honour in the line and guarded the king's tent. Seven thousand allied Greek infantry were with Alexander's army when it invaded Persia. A Macedonian general commanded this force. In addition, there were approximately 9,000 Greek mercenaries at the battle of Gaugamela. These men were equipped along traditional hoplite lines, with hoplons, bronze helmets, and armed with a spear and sword. Finally, Alexander had with him various forms of light infantry. He had a corps of archers; 1,000 Agrianian javelin men, who are described as the elite light infantry force of the army; and 7,000 other light infantry troops armed with weapons such as javelins and slings. As noted, in battle the main function of these light infantry troops was to protect the main units of the army from pre-emptive attack and, along with some of the cavalry units, to protect the flanks of the entire army. As the campaigns progressed, the Agrianians and archers play an increasingly central role in many of Alexander's operations. Alexander had a diverse army, both in terms of the types of forces and in its ethnic origins. It is to his credit that he maintained it as such an effective and cohesive organization for the length of time that he did. In his later campaigns, he made increasing use of lighter and specialized oriental units, and indeed made the entire army lighter to deal with more varied terrain and guerrilla forces. The details of these changes will be dealt with later.

The Battle of Chaeronea

As with all military innovations, those of Philip II would only be of use if they could bring victory on the battlefield. The strategic world is a very practical one, in which the test of any army is a bloody violent struggle. Bad or antiquated ideas tend to die on battlefields along with those who employ them. For Philip, the decisive test for his new instrument in pitched battle in mainland Greece was at the Battle of Chaeronea in 338. In the period before Chaeronea, Macedonia was quickly becoming the most powerful state in Greece. Militarily it could put into the field an army that would outnumber the forces of many of the other city-states combined. Nonetheless, Philip had hoped to achieve hegemonic power through peaceful means. His ambitions were resisted by states such as Athens, Thebes, and Sparta. Consequently, in August 338 the city-states of Boeotia, Athens, Thebes, Achaea, Corinth and Megara mustered a force of 35,000 at Chaeronea. To face this force of hoplites, Philip had 30,000 infantry and 2,000 cavalry. The king commanded the right wing of the army, and the young Alexander took charge of the Companion cavalry on the left. Opposite them, the Greek allies placed their strongest forces on both wings. The Thebans manned the right, whilst Philip faced the Athenian hoplites on the left wing. The inferior forces of the other city-states held the middle of the Greek line. Hanson is derisory in his description of the Greek Allied forces. He describes them as reactionary, part-time militiamen.

In a sense, Chaeronea is one of those moments in history when one side in a battle does not realize that warfare has changed. The Greek Allied forces would pay for this error with their lives. Facing these part-time warriors with their anachronistic equipment, limited tactics and incompetent generals, was a professional, well-equipped, well-motivated, combined-arms force led by two innovative commanders. A similar scene could be found in the deserts of Iraq in 1991. The Iraqi army relied on Soviet equipment and doctrine; was manned largely by conscripts; and at the highest level was commanded by a man with little operational insight. They faced an opponent manned largely by professional troops, who had developed new technologies and doctrine precisely with the aim of defeating a Soviet style army. To make matters worse for the Iraqis, the war took place in a predominately flat, open terrain that ideally suited the dominant air power of its foe. The results for both the Greek Allied forces and the Iraqis were predictable. As the Athenians advanced in predictable fashion, Philip's well-disciplined phalangites enacted a pre-planned and organized feigned retreat. This manoeuvre dragged the Athenians away from the forces in the centre of the Greek line. As this was occurring, Alexander launched his attack on the Thebans at his front and broke through their line. Just as the Athenian generals were leading their men forward in a rash and false hope for glory, in a well-timed manoeuvre the Macedonian phalanx halted, lowered its sarissae and impaled the Athenian hoplites on their spearheads. In all, the Athenians lost appoximately 1,000 men. Meanwhile, having breached the enemy's line, Alexander now turned the Companions into the rear of the Thebans and pushed them onto the oncoming pikes of the Macedonian phalanx. The Theban Sacred Band, an elite and highly motivated unit, was slain to a man.

Conclusion

Did Philip II and Alexander enact an RMA? The innovations that proved so decisive at Chaeronea appear to fulfil the main RMA criteria to varying degrees. Technologically, the changes were minimal. Although the extended length of the sarissa and cavalry spear gave the Macedonian forces increased offensive punch, in many respects the forces resembled those of the Greek city-states. And as noted, many of the reforms brought to fruition by

51

Philip had their origins in changes that had been occurring since before the Peloponnesian War. In this respect, technologically the army that Alexander took to Persia was hardly revolutionary. The big changes came in political motivation, organization and doctrine. As with Nazi Germany and Napoleonic France, the imperial ambitions of both Philip and Alexander were a great driving force that helped mould their military innovations. This helped to produce an army that was designed for campaigning year-round and in all terrains. It was also imbued with the aim of achieving crushingly decisive victories against its enemies. The quasi-ritualistic methods of traditional hoplite warfare were forgone, and replaced by warfare much more total in its aims and methods. This called for a combined-arms force that could smash an opponent's line and inflict heavy casualties in the pursuit. The relative advantage of the Macedonian forces came less from any revolutionary leap forward in technology, and more from the way this new army was utilized. This is an important point for those in the RMA/Military Transformation community that promote a technological vision of warfare. Perhaps more important still were the men who commanded the Macedonian forces. As the remaining chapters of this book will reveal, the extraordinary military successes during the invasion of the Persian Empire cannot be understood without reference to the military genius of Alexander the Great.

2

Early Tests: Rebellions at Home and the Battle of the Granicus

Operations in Greece and the Balkans

Alexander's first test as a military commander came in the immediate aftermath of his father's assassination in 336. The death of Philip II gave the Greek city-states an opportunity to rid themselves of Macedonian hegemony. The Athenian orator Demosthenes led the revolt. This was a severe test for Alexander, the newly crowned king. Alongside Athens, other significant city-states, Thebes, Argos and Thessaly, also supported the rebellion. To add insult to injury, the rebels had also opened-up relations with Darius III in Persia. Fearful that Alexander would continue with his father's invasion of his empire, Darius saw the rebellion as an opportunity to unite with the Greeks against a common enemy. To make matters worse for Alexander, Thracian tribes on his northeastern border were preparing to invade Macedonia. The enemies of Macedonia hoped and believed that the forces now lining up against

Alexander would overwhelm this relatively inexperienced young ruler. Alexander had come to the throne with many of his father's plans still incomplete. In particular, the League of Corinth was still in its infancy. Philip had established the League after his victory at Chaeronea. In essence, the League was a political union and a collective security organization amongst the Greek city-states, with Philip as its ruler. Its declared objectives were to maintain peace and stability between the Greek states. However, in reality it protected governments loyal to Philip within the Greek states and provided legitimacy to Macedonian hegemony. For the war with Persia, the League of Corinth also provided Macedonia with a ready-made alliance from which to obtain forces. Beyond Greece, the Balkans had not been wholly pacified, and the campaign in Persia was in its early stages. However, rather than be overwhelmed as his opponents hoped, Alexander used the situation to cement his rule in Greece and to create a secure home base from which to launch his invasion of Persia.

Faced with such an array of enemies, Alexander had to move rapidly before the various threats could coalesce into an insurmountable whole. The rapidity of his operations would become one of the hallmarks of Alexander's successful style of warfare. In this vein, Alexander led his army swiftly southwards and entered Thessaly. The Thessalians barred his way at the Tempe Pass. In this first test of his generalship Alexander proved himself to be not just an expert in the application of brute force on the battlefield, but also a master of manoeuvre. Rather than attempt to storm the pass, he had his troops cut footholds into the face of Mount Ossa, and thereby was able to circumvent the enemy's defences. When the Macedonian army appeared in their rear the Thessalians submitted without a fight. As a result, the Thessalians confirmed Alexander as the President of the Thessalian League and supplied him with a force of their outstanding cavalry. Throughout his career Alexander would prove time and again that he was able to outwit his opponents so dramatically that often manoeuvre was enough to attain victory. From here Alexander pushed on into central Greece. Again, the speed of his advance caught his enemies off guard. With his forces encamped outside Thebes, just 64 km (40 miles) from Athens, the Athenians submitted to his rule. With that, the rebellion in Greece ended and Alexander was proclaimed Hegemon of the League of Corinth for life. He was also appointed as the Captain-General of the war of revenge against Persia. This was a significant political victory for Alexander. By gaining the declared support of the League of Corinth, Alexander could promote his campaigns in Persia as being officially in the interests of the wider Greek world.

Despite the support he now enjoyed from the League of Corinth, Alexander was still loath to embark on his invasion of Persia without securing the northern borders of Macedonia. Alexander planned to leave an army under the command of his general, Antipater, to guard the home base whilst he campaigned in Asia. The king's main concern was that the Balkan tribes, who were still planning to revolt against him, might find a willing Greek ally in Sparta. Sparta was not a member of the League of Corinth, and was therefore somewhat outside Alexander's sphere of domination in Greece. A rebellion that combined the Balkan tribes with an ally in Greece might prove too much for Antipater and his force. The main area of concern was the land between Macedonia and the river Danube. It was in this locale that troublesome tribes such as the Triballians, Illyrians and Getae resided. Alexander's aim was to subdue the area north of Macedonia up to the Danube, and use the great river as a secure frontier to his empire. Consequently, in the spring of 335 Alexander headed north to subdue the tribes of Thrace. There is conflicting evidence concerning the size of the army he took with him into Thrace. The figures range from 15,000 to 30,000. However, whatever the size of the army it contained some of Alexander's best forces, including the phalangites, hypaspists, Agrianians, archers and the Companion cavalry. The army was a combined-arms force, and at its core were the nationalistic and professional Macedonians.

The first resistance Alexander met came from local tribesmen and Thracian troops on a pass over Mount Haemus. Again, there is some debate over the actual pass in question. Many authors name it as the Shipka Pass, although Bosworth claims that it may have been the Trojan Pass. The Free Thracians had blockaded the pass with wagons at its steepest point. Their plan was to release the wagons down the pass, and thereby not only inflict casualties on Alexander's men, but also to break up the phalanx and then engage the phalangites individually. However, as was so often the case, Alexander had identified his opponent's intentions and put in place a counter-measure. As the wagons rumbled down the pass, on Alexander's orders the phalanx opened its ranks in disciplined fashion to allow the wagons to pass harmlessly through. Where this was not possible, the troops were instructed to lay flat and lock their shields together covering themselves, so that the wagons might roll over them with little damage. The Thracians had played their trump card, and had failed to take Alexander's men out of the game. Now came the Macedonian response. Again, there is some confusion over the details of the battle that followed. Some accounts place the phalanx as the lead unit in the advance. In such accounts the phalanx receives supporting fire from archers on their right and support from the hypaspists and Agrianians on the left. In contrast, some of the literature identifies the Agrianians and hypaspists as the lead units, with the phalanx following close behind. In such terrain, and with the enemy fleeing the area of battle, it seems most likely that the more lightly armed and mobile forces, such as the hypaspists, would be better suited to lead the attack. In any case, whichever units led the assault, the lightly armed Thracian troops and tribesmen fled down the pass. Still, 1,500 of them were killed in the action. A number of women and children were captured and sent to Macedonia.

Having dealt with this small contingent in the pass, Alexander continued his march north to deal with Syrmus, King of the Triballians. However, as he headed towards the Danube Alexander suddenly found that a force of Triballians had marched onto his rear. This would not be the last time that Alexander would be surprised by such a manoeuvre. He would find himself in a similar position, a little less than three years later, at Issus in November 333. On this occasion, the Macedonian army outmanoeuvred its Triballian foe and surprised them at their camp in a dense wooded glen. However, despite his clever operational manoeuvre, Alexander faced a problem. The wooded glen was too dense to allow an organized and cohesive frontal attack. To bring his forces to bear, Alexander needed to draw the Triballians out into the open. This has always been the main problem for a regular army facing an irregular foe: how to compel them into an open engagement. Like many great commanders, Alexander was astute at playing upon the psychological make-up of his opponents. He also displayed an early example of his ability to utilize a combined-arms force in such circumstances. In this instance, he used his slingers and archers as bait. They harassed the enemy forces hidden within the glen. The Triballians played right into Alexander's hands and came forward to deal with his missile troops. As they came into the open, Alexander led the phalanx against the enemy's centre. As the centre was breached, enemy cavalry squadrons outflanked the Triballians on both wings. This simple ruse led to the slaughter of 3,000 Triballian troops, for the loss of only 40 Macedonian infantrymen and 11 cavalrymen. These outstanding kill ratios would become another telling hallmark of Alexander's campaigns.

With Alexander rapidly approaching the Danube, King Syrmus had retreated with his people to the island of Peuce in the middle of the great river. Before setting off on his Balkan campaign Alexander had sent an advance force of warships up the Danube. Although much of his campaigning would be done inland, Alexander rarely missed the opportunity to use naval forces for logistic support. As in this case, this often included the use of riverine craft. In this sense, Alexander's appreciation of joint operations between land and naval forces has perhaps sometimes been underappreciated. His riverine and land forces now joined together for an assault on the island. Macedonian forces boarded the ships and headed for an amphibious assault on the island. However, the tide was strong and the potential landing sights were well defended by the Triballians. In these circumstances an opposed amphibious landing by such a small force as the ships could carry may have proved extremely costly. The attack was abandoned.

However, with his enemy isolated in the middle of the Danube, Alexander could begin devastating their lands, and thereby, hopefully starve them into submission. The crops were almost ready for harvesting, and so they represented a valuable target. In this respect, Alexander revealed an early example of his astute grasp of the art of coercion. An enemy can be defeated in a number of ways, depending on one's objectives. On occasions, the enemy's forces and resources will need to be physically destroyed to achieve one's strategic goals. However, often victory can be gained through the limited or threatened use of force to compel the enemy to accede to one's demands. In these cases the primary target is the mind of the opposing commander, and physical force is the medium through which that mind is influenced. In a classic example of such a strategy Alexander constructed a plan to coerce King Syrmus. His plans received a welcome and significant boost with the arrival of a force of Getae on the northern bank of the Danube. This Thracian tribe had deployed 10,000 infantry and 4,000 cavalry in the hope of deterring the Macedonian king from crossing the river into their territory. For Alexander, the Getae force

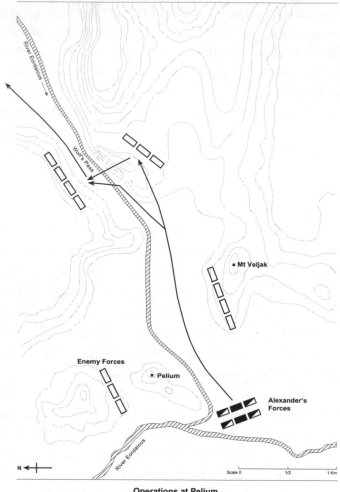

Operations at Pelium

represented both a threat and an opportunity. Such a force would complicate his coercive operations against the Triballians, and indeed could offer aide to the forces on Peuce. However, a crushing victory over the Getae could add substantially to his campaign of coercion. Of course, the main military challenge for Alexander was how to cross such a wide and powerful river in the face of an enemy force of 14,000. Alexander's answer to this challenge was innovative and decisive. His forces constructed log canoes and stuffed hides for the crossing. Together with his warships, these platforms enabled Alexander to cross the river with 4,000 infantry and 1,500 cavalry, at night and away from the Getae. To further conceal his intentions, Alexander landed his forces amongst the cornfields. At dawn, the Macedonians launched their attack on the unsuspecting Getae. Nicanor led the phalanx along the riverbank to protect the flank of the army. Alexander led the cavalry in a series of charges with the squadrons in wedge formation. The Getae fled the area, leaving their main settlement open to attack. The Getae town was looted and razed. This innovative and decisive show of force produced outstanding results for Alexander. Many tribes from a wide area came forward and submitted themselves to Macedonian rule. More importantly, King Syrmus did the same. Alexander had pacified some of the most troublesome Balkan tribes in this one operation without the loss of a single man. However, his Balkan adventure was not over yet. Two Illyrian chiefs, Cleitus and Glaucias, rose to challenge Macedonian hegemony.

Cleitus, the son of an old Macedonian enemy Bardylis, had allied with Glaucias, King of the Taulantii, and planned to invade Macedonia. It also seemed that the Autariatae, in modern day Bosnia, had a role to play in this revolt by attacking Alexander's forces as they marched to engage the two Illyrian chiefs. To deal with this latter threat Alexander sent his ally King Langarus of the Agrianians to attack the forces of the Autariatae. This would protect the flank of Alexander's army as they marched to Pelium, a fortified city that Cleitus was occupying on the border with Macedonia. Pelium was to be the base of operations for the invasion of Alexander's kingdom. To the surprise of Cleitus, Alexander's army arrived at Pelium before Cleitus had been able to join forces with the army of Glaucias. When Alexander arrived in the area the bulk of Cleitus' men were deployed on a ring of hills around Pelium. As the Macedonian forces approached the city, sections of the enemy came down from the hills and launched an attack. There are precious few details about this engagement, but it is reported that Cleitus' men received a severe mauling from the Macedonians. Consequently, the positions on the hills were abandoned, and Alexander was now able to begin his siege of the fortified city. However, war being the realm of the unexpected, Alexander had to abandon his plans for a siege when on the following day the army of Glaucias arrived in the locale. Alexander's forces were insufficient to both assault the city and fend-off the expected attack from Glaucias' considerable army. Consequently, Alexander had to retreat to his fortified camp next to the river Eordaicus and consider his next move. Glaucias' army, with the remnants of Cleitus' men from the previous day's engagement, had reoccupied positions on the surrounding hills. Alexander was facing a desperate situation. Not only was he heavily outnumbered; his options were becoming increasingly limited by his logistical demands. Alexander was rapidly running short of supplies for his army. He had to act quickly. To solve his supply problem he dispatched Philotas with cavalry and horse-drawn wagons to gather food. Not surprisingly,

Glaucias seized upon this opportunity to defeat a section of Alexander's army in detail, and manoeuvred onto the hills surrounding the plain from which the supplies would be drawn. The Macedonian king acted quickly to this threat and led a force of hypaspists, cavalry, archers and Agrianians to rescue Philotas and his men. Alexander's precarious position is clearly evident from this episode. In the first instance he had to risk a section of his force to gather crucial supplies despite the obvious risks. It quickly became apparent just how vulnerable Philotas' detachment was. So, Alexander was left with little choice but to rescue Philotas' force, whilst at the same time having to leave a sufficient army in place to deter the forces inside Pelium from venturing out to join with Glaucias' men. In the end, Alexander managed to balance these various needs and threats. Glaucias' men did not risk an attack on Philotas' detachment. Nor did the forces in Pelium attempt a breakout. Yet, despite this limited success, the respite was short-lived. The episode must have made it apparent that Alexander could not risk another such move to gather supplies. He would have to devise a more permanent solution to his predicament.

As we will see in the coming chapters, one of the notable features of Alexander's three great battles against Persian forces was the offensive charge led by the Companion cavalry. However, as a commander Alexander had much greater variety to his art. As he stood outside Pelium, short of supplies and with his enemies deployed on the hills around him, it became clear that he would have to affect a clever tactical withdrawal. The most sensible route for this retreat presented a number of obstacles. The main danger would come from enemy forces deployed on the foothills along the route of his withdrawal. This danger increased dramatically as the route passed through the narrow Wolf's Pass, which was dominated by a steep-sided hill. To make matters even worse, the river Eordaicus ran through the pass and would have to be forded in the face of the enemy. So, Alexander's first task was to remove the enemy from the foothills along the initial section of his route of advance. His solution to this problem was innovative, although similar to the actions of Epaminondas at Mantinea in 362 BC. Alexander's forces were deployed on a plain, with the enemy deployed on the foothills to the north and south of his position. The Taulantii mainly held the northern foothills, in which Pelium was situated, whilst the Dardanians occupied the southern hills. The tactic Alexander utilized for this action relied primarily upon the coercive effects that a professional well-trained army could produce. He deployed the phalanx on the open plain in close formation with a depth of 120 men. Squadrons of cavalry protected the flanks of this force. The phalangites then went through a series of well-drilled manoeuvres in clear view of the enemy. Their first movement, which they performed in the spearhead formation, was aimed towards the Dardanians on Mount Veljak. As the enemy retreated from the foothills in the face of this apparent advance, their fellow Illyrians on the northern foothills launched an assault on the rear of the phalanx. However, with great tactical precision the phalangites did an about turn, let out a battle cry and clashed their pikes against their shields. Faced with such a cohesive force of phalangites and cavalry, the Taulantians fled back to and over the northern hills.

The success of these manoeuvres has raised doubts about

whether the phalanx employed the sarissa in the Balkans. It is claimed that such complex manoeuvring could not have been carried out whilst brandishing a 4.8m- (16-ft) pike. Likewise, the author of this theory, Markle, notes how difficult it would be to bang such a pike against the small shield of the phalangite. Markle admits that Alexander's men entered the Balkans with sarissae, but questions whether they used them in such combat situations. There does appear to be a degree of logic in Markle's argument, and thus it deserves our attention. However, the coercive affect of the phalanx manoeuvres would not have so dramatic on the enemy had Alexander's men been armed in the traditional hoplite fashion. On the other hand, regardless of the armaments, it may simply have been a combination of the cohesion and discipline of Alexander's combined-arms force that produced the coercive effect. Once again Alexander had achieved a challenging tactical objective without the need to engage the enemy in combat.

Alexander had cleared the first obstacle to the withdrawal of his forces. He now faced the task of clearing the enemy off the hill overlooking Wolf's Pass. Having just showed an extraordinary degree of tactical finesse, Alexander now relied upon a frontal assault of the enemy. The king led his seven personal bodyguards and personal Companions in an attack against the enemy on the hill dominating the pass. This elite and highly motivated force of cavalry was prepared for a tough fight, which could have included dismounted combat. However, in the event the enemy fled before contact could be made. Despite their relative numerical advantage, the enemy had once again proved to be no match for Alexander's men in spirit. Once he had a foothold on the hill, Alexander quickly reinforced his position with 2,000 Agrianians and archers. With the hill secure, the rest of the army could begin to withdraw across the river in Wolf's Pass. The force forded the river with the hypaspists taking the lead. With the majority of his army now forming line on the far side of the river, the Taulantians moved to engage Alexander and his men who were still holding position on the hill. Once again, the enemy had spotted an opportunity to engage a fraction of Alexander's army and attempted to defeat it in detail. Alexander acted with typical speed and attacked the oncoming enemy with his cavalry. At the same time, some of his phalangites feigned a re-crossing of the river to threaten the flank of the Taulantians. Again, the enemy did not stand in the face of this assault. Once the threat from the Taulantians had receded Alexander led the Agrianians and archers across the river. Finally, the Companions and Bodyguards began to cross the river. To cover this final crossing Alexander had the archers and his field catapults pin-down the remaining enemy forces. Not a single man had been lost in this tactical withdrawal.

For the next three days Alexander's men were able to re-supply in safety in the Ventrok and Prespa basins. However, the battle with the Illyrians was not yet over. Having been on the defensive, the Macedonian king now turned the tide on his adversaries. Despite their inability to inflict any damage on Alexander's army, Cleitus and Glaucias had concluded the actions around Pelium imbued with a false sense of security. They believed that Alexander had continued on his retreat from the theatre of operations and was returning to Macedonia. Instead, Alexander had reccived intelligence that the cnemy was camped outside of their fortifications without any real defences or security measures. Alexander now returned to the area he had previously withdrawn from, and took with him the hypaspists, Agrianians, archers and brigades of phalangites. The attack came at night, and completely caught the enemy by surprise. Many were captured or killed as they slept. Cleitus fell back on Pelium. Meanwhile, thc Taulantians fled, only to be pursued for 100 km (62 miles) by Alexander at the head of his cavalry. Eventually, Cleitus accepted that the planned invasion of Macedonia would not occur. As if to signal this, he burnt Pelium and abandoned the area. The Illyrian threat to Macedonia was over. Indeed, the Illyrians provided troops for the invasion of Persia in 334. In many respects, Alexander's campaign in the Balkans ranks alongside many of his later achievements. Alexander had gained the submission of a number of rebellious tribes, and thereby pacified a large area of territory, with minimal losses to his own forces and very little actual combat. On so many occasions, his tactical and operational manoeuvring had undone his enemies. This skill would serve him well in the Persian Empire. However, in the later campaigns he would also show that he had a keen ability to know when, and how, to inflict devastating defeats on the battlefield.

The good news for Alexander was that he had secured the northern frontier of Macedonia; the bad news was that rebellion had erupted again in Greecc. Darius III had been supplying and bribing the enemies of Alexander with gold. A rumour had been started that Alexander had been killed in the

Balkans. This strengthened the resolve of those wishing to free themselves from Macedonian hegemony. The city of Thebes took the lead in the rebellion and besieged the Macedonian garrison in the Theban citadel of Cadmeia. At Athens, Demosthenes persuaded the city to assist Thebes in its action. When news of this uprising reached Alexander he was still near Pelium, some 482 km (300 miles) from Thebes. Again, speed would be his greatest weapon. He force marched his army and within thirteen days had reached Boeotia. The rapid pace of his advance prevented any other forces coming to the aid of Thebes. The Thebans now stood isolated with the forces of Alexander outside their city. Rather than invest the city for a long period, Alexander launched a series of assaults upon its walls. Despite fierce resistance, which led to the deaths of 500 Macedonians, the defences were eventually breached. A massacre ensued, in which 6,000 Thebans were killed. In order to deter future rebellions Alexander decided to make an example of Thebes. He had the city destroyed and the remaining 30,000 citizens enslaved. However, in contrast his treatment of Athens was merciful. This leniency was not motivated by some moral code; rather it was a logical strategic decision. Athens was central to Greek culture, and Alexander needed her naval forces for the war with Persia. Letting Athens off the hook would help maintain the cohesion of the League of Corinth. With the violent crushing of the Theban revolt, Alexander had finally completed his operations to secure his home base. He could now prepare his army for the invasion of the Persian Empire.

The Invasion Begins: The Battle of the Granicus

Before Alexander could lead the army into Asia he had to organize the security of Macedonia and Greece in his absence. Having worked so hard to establish a secure base before he left, it would be catastrophic if serious rebellion were to flare-up whilst he was campaigning in Asia. Thus, he left Antipater, Philip's top diplomat and a crucial supporter in Alexander's claim to the throne, as his deputy Hegemon. Antipater was given command of a substantial force of 12,000 phalangites, 1,000 Companion cavalry, 500 light cavalry and other light infantry units. With the arrangements in Macedonia complete, Alexander led the army of 40,000 frontline troops a distance of 500 km (310 miles) to the Hellespont in just twenty days. Following the invasion route of Xerxes in 480, Alexander chose to cross at Sestos. There, the fleet, comprising 160 warships and accompanying supply vessels, joined the army for the crossing to Abydus. For the Greeks of this period religious symbolism and the support of the gods were crucial for any military campaign. Before the crossing was made, Alexander had twelve altars erected to the Olympian gods. Then, as the forces crossed the narrow straits, a bull was sacrificed onboard the flagship and libations poured into the water to honour Poseidon and the Nereids. Finally, as the ships approached the opposite shoreline, Alexander leapt ashore in full parade armour and drove his spear into the ground declaring: 'I accept from the gods Asia won by spear.' This symbolic act made clear both Alexander's intent and the method by which he would pursue it.

However, an even more impressive act of symbolism

was to come. Alexander was a devotee of Homer's *Iliad*, and he intended to pay tribute to the heroes of the Trojan War. With the main body of the army still completing the crossing, Alexander moved south from the landing site to visit the tomb of Achilles. There, to honour the great hero, he laid a wreath on the tomb, and with his Companions engaged in the traditional act of naked racing. From here, Alexander moved to Troy itself. In the temple of Athena Alexander dedicated his armour, and was shown weapons that dated back to the Trojan War. Amongst them were said to be those of Achilles himself. To summon the support of these great Greek heroes of the past, Alexander took the shield of Achilles and replaced it with his own. Such symbolic acts as these may seem anachronistic to modern eyes, yet they fulfilled a number of significant purposes for Alexander and his men. On the one hand, they served a very pragmatic propaganda function for the young king. By aligning himself with great Greek heroes of the past, Alexander was further able to sell his campaigns as serving the interests of the wider Greek Community. They also served important military functions. Military forces are not merely anodyne units to be moved around on the battle-field; they are social organizations in which morale and culture play a central role. By pleasing the gods and aligning the coming campaigns with the great exploits of the past, Alexander was helping to maintain morale and engender a broader sense of purpose amongst his forces. Alexander was an astute commander and strategist. However, we must not forget that Alexander was human as well, and therefore prone to his own emotions and personal desires. In this sense, these acts may well have been motivated by an egocentric sense of his place in history. Whatever the true motivation, with these symbolic acts completed the army was now prepared for the first big test in the field against the forces of the Persian Empire.

With the army now across the Hellespont, Alexander moved rapidly. His crossing had been unopposed, largely because the Macedonian vanguard, although driven back by the much-heralded Greek mercenary general Memnon, remained in control of the crossing points on the Hellespont. Also, the substantial Persian fleet had not yet entered the Aegean to harass Alexander. Within three days he was in the Granicus plain, taking with him mainly his elite Macedonian forces numbering 13,000 infantry and 5,100 cavalry. Faced with the young king and his invasion force the Persian commanders had been considering two options. Memnon put forward a 'scorched-earth' policy. This plan seemed to hold a great deal of promise. Alexander was running short of supplies, and in the pre-harvest period the burning of the crops would leave the invading Macedonian ruler few supplies with which to feed his men. Understandably, the local satraps (provincial governors), led by Arsites (Satrap of Hellespontine–Phrygia), baulked at the prospect of devastating their own lands. There was also an element of distrust of the Greek mercenary Memnon amongst the other Persian generals. The alternative option was to risk an early pitched battle with Alexander. The problem with this option was the relative inferiority of the Persian infantry. Neither option looked especially inviting. Nonetheless, with the enemy now in their territory, a decision had to be made. However, the process of decision making amongst the Persian high command was cumbersome and problematic. Amongst the multiple commanders there was no clear hierarchy of authority. The result of this process was that policy was decided on the basis of a majority vote.

The process by which strategic decisions are made is crucial. It is not only important that the right decision is made, but that the right decision is made and acted upon quickly enough. The American World War Two commander General George Patton captures this truism well when he stated that 'a good plan violently executed now is better than a perfect plan next week.' The Persians had a number of problems in this respect. Not only was their decision-making process slow and cumbersome, it was also liable to produce very average decisions. The nineteenth-century general and theorist Baron Antoine Henri de Jomini convincingly claims that decisions made by committee are often limited to the lowest common denominator. For Jomini, the ideal was to have the decision-making process centralized in the hands of a military genius like his own commander-in-chief, Napoleon. The combination of mental and moral characteristics required for outstanding command is rare. This ensures that military geniuses are few and far between. Unfortunately for the Persians, they were facing one of these rare creatures in Alexander. As we have already seen in the Greek and Balkan campaigns, Alexander had the ability to make the right decision and act upon it quickly. This was true at the tactical, operational and strategic levels of war. The process by which decisions are made can be expressed through the 'OODA Loop'. This theory describes the sequence of actions through which decisions are made relative to the enemy. First comes *observation* of the situation; then one *orientates* oneself; makes a *decision*; and finally *acts* upon it. This idea was first developed by Colonel John Boyd as an analytical tool for understanding the tactical performance of fighter pilots in dogfights. However, it quickly became apparent that the OODA Loop was applicable across all of the levels of war. As we progress through Alexander's campaigns, we will see that in most circumstances his OODA Loop operated more quickly than his opponents, and therefore he can be said to be operating inside the decision cycle of his enemies. This produces a result in which Alexander has the initiative and therefore to a large degree is able to dictate the flow of the battle.

Through their awkward decision-making process the Persians rejected Memnon's advice and made the decision to face Alexander in a pitched battle. It is easy in retrospect to criticise the decision to face Alexander in battle with forces of inferior quality. However, on balance it was probably worth a gamble. The Persians had never faced Alexander in the field, and therefore they had no direct experience of his qualities as a commander. In addition, the Persians had enjoyed some substantial successes against the Macedonian vanguard force in 335. The Macedonian campaign in Asia had started well in 336 during Philip's reign. The presence of Philip's forces had encouraged a series of democratic rebellions against Persian rule in the occupied Greek cities. However, towards the end of 336 Memnon, in command of mercenary forces, began to turn the tide in the war and gradually reduced the area under Macedonian influence. His successes included the defeat of a numerically superior force at Magnesia. On the back of these successes there was a mobilization of the satrapies in Asia Minor, and so Persian forces in the region began to increase in number and concentrate their efforts. Outnumbered, the

Macedonian commander Calas was forced to retreat towards the Hellespont. Thus, although the Persians understood that the arrival of Alexander's forces represented the main Macedonian invasion, the successes of 335 must have given them a degree of confidence for the coming battles. In such circumstances, it does not seem unreasonable to chance one's arm against the invading forces under the command of a young king who was something of an unknown quantity.

However, there was another compelling reason to seek an early battle, and that was to prevent Alexander from establishing himself in the Persian Empire. Left alone, Alexander would be able to gather local support to his cause and establish military infrastructure such as bases of operation and lines of communication. Whereas an early setback for Alexander might dissuade the locals from accepting his hegemony, and more importantly might break the cohesion of the League of Corinth in its support of the campaign. It was clear from events in the previous year that there was a degree of dissatisfaction with Alexander's rule within Greece. Ill-founded rumours of Alexander's death in the Balkans had been enough to inspire a rebellion amongst the Greek city-states; a defeat in battle may have the same effect. With the resources of an entire empire at their disposal, the Persians could risk an army in an early attempt to bring Alexander's invasion to a premature conclusion.

After concentrating their forces at Zelea, the Persian commanders decided to make their stand against Alexander on the eastern side of the river Granicus. The Granicus was a steep-sided stream sourced from Mount Ida. Conscious of the inferiority of their infantry forces relative to Alexander's, the Persians needed a strong defensive position. The Granicus

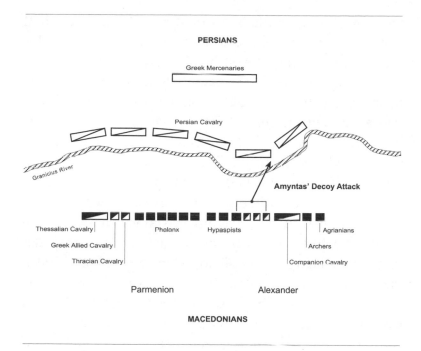

The Battle of the Granicus

was a good choice for the Persians in that it held a number of operational and tactical advantages. In the first instance it drew Alexander away from Sardis; blocked the approach to the Asian Gates, a pass through which the eastward road ran; and could not be turned on either flank. At the tactical level, although the river could be forded in places, its steep banks afforded a good defensive platform to operate from. It has been estimated that the banks would have been 3–4 m (9–13 ft) in height at the time of the battle. Such an obstacle could potentially dislocate the mighty Macedonian phalanx as it advanced on the waiting Persians. For the Persians, disrupting the Macedonian phalanx was always going to be a prime consideration in any battle with Alexander. The phalanx was

75

the foundation upon which Alexander's battle plan rested. If that solid tactical base could be broken, then the rest of his forces became vulnerable on their flanks and in the rear.

Alexander arrived at the battlefield in mid-to-late afternoon. There then ensued a famous exchange between Alexander and his second in command, Parmenion. The latter, conscious of the strong defensive characteristics of the enemy's position, advised against an attack before nightfall. Parmenion hoped that this pause would give the Persians time to withdraw. However, Alexander had noticed a flaw in the Persians' position and wished to exploit it before it was too late. At the Granicus Alexander faced an infantry force of approximately 20,000 Greek mercenaries, and a cavalry force of similar size. Whilst the infantry were not particularly renowned, the Persian cavalry were excellent. This elite force was drawn from across the empire and was commanded by members of Darius' family and entourage: 'The Kinsmen'.

The flaw that had attracted Alexander's attention related to the disposition of the Persian forces. There has been much speculation about both the dispositions of the Persian forces at the Granicus, and the reasons for such a deployment. The most obvious deployment for the Persians would have been to place the heavy infantry at the top of the riverbank, so as to meet the Macedonian forces with a solid line of spears and take advantage of the higher ground. Their cavalry should have been kept in reserve on the open plains behind the river. Their role would have been to mount a charge against any of Alexander's forces that broke through the Persian lines along the riverbank. In fact, the actual deployment was the exact reverse. The elite Persian cavalry was placed on top of the bank, with the Greek mercenaries held back in reserve. One theory put forward for this decision is based on social factors. Fuller claims that a sense of social superiority compelled the cavalry to take pride of place at the front of the defensive position. However, a more compelling rationale was that the Persian generals, fielding an inferior force, and realizing the significance of Alexander to the entire invasion campaign, focused their plan on killing the young Macedonian king. The best way to achieve this seemed to be to place their best forces at the front. And in this case, the cavalry also seemed best able to deal with the Companion cavalry, which Alexander would inevitably lead himself. Whatever the reason for this tactical error, Alexander had noticed it, and moved swiftly to take advantage of the immobilization of the Greek mercenaries.

Across the river from the Persians Alexander drew up his forces in the following order. The six battalions of the phalanx took the centre. To the right of the phalanx where one of the key components of Alexander's combined-arms tactics: Nicanor's hypaspists. Moving further to the right, alongside Nicanor's forces was a combined force under Amyntas. This consisted of lancers (prodromoi), Paeonian light horse, and an ile of the Companion cavalry. A battalion of hypaspists, the 'Royal Brigade', strengthened this force. Completing the right wing of the army were the Companion cavalry, and finally archers under Clearchus and the Agrianians under Attalus. To the left of the six central battalions of the phalanx Parmenion commanded the Thracian, Greek, and Thessalian cavalry. In all, Alexander fielded a force of approximately 13,000 infantry and 5,000 cavalry. His line stretched for 4 km (2.5 miles).

As the two forces faced each other across the river, the Persians expected Alexander to attack the left of their line. Instead, Alexander would focus his main effort on the Persians' centre left. However, before Alexander led the Companion cavalry in the decisive assault, he needed to deceive the Persians of his real intent and draw some of the elite Persian cavalry away from the centre. This is where Amyntas' force played its crucial, and costly role. The objective given to Amyntas was to cross the river and attack up the bank towards the left of the Persian line. With this assault Amyntas would hopefully stretch the Persian line to the left and occupy the attention of the enemy's cavalry in that sector. This operation would then prevent those Persian forces engaged from interfering with the crossing of Alexander's forces towards the centre left of the Persian line. This was a crucial undertaking. Perhaps the greatest threat to Alexander's plan was that his forces could be mauled whilst trying to ford the river. Therefore, Amyntas had been given a great deal of responsibility. However, with this honour came the knowledge that he was vastly outnumbered and faced the cream of the Persian cavalry under the command of Memnon himself. In addition to these disadvantages, Amyntas was initially fighting from the river itself and up an incline towards his enemy. Not surprisingly the Persian spears inflicted heavy casualties on the Macedonians. Nonetheless, Amyntas' men did their job and left the way open for the main effort.

In line with the heroic tradition of the times, Alexander led the assault on the Persians' centre left and was bedecked in his finery. In particular, brilliant white plumes billowing from his helmet distinguished him from his men. The start of the attack was heralded by the blast of trumpets and shouts of 'Engalius', the Homeric Greek god of war. Alexander and his Royal Squadron led the Companion cavalry in the attack. With them were two battalions of hypaspists and three battalions of the phalanx. The king led his forces in an oblique charge at the enemy. Initially, as the two forces clashed the battle resembled a close infantry struggle, albeit conducted with cavalry forces. In this bloody struggle Alexander's men had the aims of pushing the Persian cavalry back from the riverbank, and then creating a bridgehead. In contrast, the Persians sought to force the Macedonians back into the river where they could slaughter them. Although the terrain was against the Macedonians, they had some significant compensatory advantages. Aside from Alexander himself, they had a distinct technological edge over their foe. The Persian cavalry were armed with short javelins. These proved to be no match for the cornel-wood spears they faced.

The battle of the Granicus provides us with an early example of both the advantages and limitations inherent in Alexander's style of command. From a cultural perspective the young king had to risk his own life by directly leading the assault. This was perhaps particularly important for a Macedonian ruler who had faced early opposition in Greece to his rule. However, Alexander very nearly paid the ultimate price for his heroic leadership on that summer afternoon at the Granicus. His distinctiveness on the battlefield certainly fired the morale of his own men, but it also made him an obvious and tempting target for his foes. In classical battles the slaying of a ruler would often signal defeat. On this occasion, during the close quarter combat Alexander had already gone through two spears before he was presented with a third by Demaratus the Corinthian. Upon receiving his new weapon Alexander noticed Mithridates (the son-in-law of Darius) leading a wedge of cavalry in his direction. Immediately, Alexander engaged, and felled Mithridates with a blow to the face. Alexander was now in the thick of the battle. As he dispatched Mithridates, Rhoesaces, another Persian leader, struck Alexander on the head with a scimitar, shearing-off part of his helmet. Now fighting for his very survival, and perhaps that of the entire campaign, Alexander swiftly turned and thrust Rhoesaces through the breast with his spear. In the melee, another Persian general, Spithridates, was behind Alexander and raised his scimitar to slay the Macedonian king. At that very moment, luck played its part. Seconds from death, Alexander was saved by Cleitus the Black, commander of the Royal Squadron, who struck Spithridates and severed his sword-arm. Not only had Alexander been saved, but it had brought the battle to its decisive moment. The loss of these divisional leaders decapitated the Persian command and control, and dealt a severe blow to the entire Persian force. The Persian centre began to collapse in the face of the assault. In response, the wings of the Persian force also began to flee the field of battle.

In the original accounts of the battle there is little mention of the forces under Parmenion on the Macedonian left. However, it seems that these forces had successfully held the flanking Persian cavalry in that sector of the battlefield. As the battle drew to its climax, with the majority of the Persian forces fleeing the battlefield, the Greek mercenaries in Persian employ stood their ground and asked for quarter.

Alexander, conscious of the need to assert his authority and deter those Greeks tempted to fight for the Persians in the future, refused their request. Instead, he ordered the hypaspists and phalanx to launch a frontal assault whilst the cavalry attacked the flank and rear. During this final melee Alexander's horse was killed under him; again demonstrating the risks of his approach to leadership. Nonetheless, of the 20,000 mercenaries engaged, 18,000 were killed and the remaining 2,000 were sent back to Macedonia as slaves. The records of the total losses are somewhat vague in the historical sources. However, the most reliable sources indicate that Persian losses were limited due to the fact that there was no pursuit. Nonetheless, their cavalry losses were still 1,000. This compares to Macedonian losses of 25 Companions, 60 other cavalry, and 30 infantrymen. The most significant losses for the Persians were those among their leaders, of whom the most significant were Spithridates, Satrap of Lydia; Mithrobazarnes, Satrap of Cappadocia; Mithridates, son-in-law of Darius; and Omares, commander of the mercenaries. After the battle, Arsites, Satrap of Hellespontine-Phrygia, committed suicide. In the aftermath of the victory Alexander's leadership skills and statesmanship are again evident. He made a point of visiting the wounded troops and allowed them to recount their heroic deeds to him. He also sent 300 sets of Persian armour to Greece and had them dedicated to Athena on the Acropolis. The purpose behind this gesture was probably to help the broader Greek Community to feel included in the victory, as well as to partially fulfil his promise of revenge on Persia.

Granicus: The Assessment

There are a number of factors that may explain Alexander's victory at the Granicus. We can look to the initial Persian mistake of deploying their cavalry along the riverbank. However, whilst there is some validity in criticising such a deployment, if the Persian plan was indeed designed to slay Alexander by facing him with their elite forces, then clearly it very nearly succeeded. Nonetheless, we can say that the chosen deployment did mean that once the first line had been breached there was no cavalry to charge the Macedonians at pace and drive them back into the river. This meant that the Greek mercenaries essentially played no role in deciding the outcome of the battle. In contrast, once the Persian cavalry had been defeated, the Greek mercenaries were left isolated and had to await their fate. Persian tactics at the Granicus were in sharp contrast to the combined-arms operations of the Macedonians.

Clearly, much of the victory can be attributed to Alexander's military genius and the forces at his disposal. Particularly worthy of note is Alexander's deception of the enemy. By stretching the Persian line to the left with Amyntas' attack, he had opened the door for the decisive assault on the centre left of the enemy's line. However, such a deception will only be profitable if you can act before the enemy can readjust and counter your main effort. For this, Alexander's forces were ideally designed. His forces exhibited remarkable speed at both the operational and tactical levels. On this occasion, Alexander acted with such speed that he was able to deal with the cavalry and infantry separately, and indeed deal with different sectors of the

Persian front line in turn. All of these manoeuvres were only possible through the proficiency in the coordination of combined-arms tactics. Obviously, the Companion cavalry could advance rapidly. However, the integrity of the Macedonian line was ensured by the hypaspists and the discipline of the phalanx. The hypaspists were able to maintain tactical contact with both the cavalry and phalanx battalions. Together, these two infantry units ensured that the enemy were not presented with gaps in the Macedonian line that they could exploit. The result was a rapid, cohesive and continuous assault on the Persian line. Finally, we should draw attention to Alexander's *coup d'oeil*. In military terms, this refers to the ability of a general to quickly perceive the decisive point and/or moment in a battle. At the Granicus Alexander had noted the vulnerability in the disposition of the Persian forces. He had also identified the decisive point in the Persian line at which his main attack would be targeted. However, in order to be able to exploit this point fully, he had to expose it with Amyntas' assault on the Persian left. Once Amyntas' men were engaged, Alexander had to choose the right moment at which to launch his own attack. Too early, and the plan would be revealed before the enemy had committed forces to the left; too late and the enemy cavalry on the left would have time to deal with Amyntas and then rejoin in the defence of the centre. Alexander seemed to get his timing just right, for the enemy centre collapsed fairly rapidly, and with it the entire Persian line. In the first battle-field test in Asia, the commander and his army had worked effectively with each other. Things would not go as smoothly in their next big tests.

3

Conquering the Coast: Bloody Sieges and the Battle of Issus

Alexander's victory at the Granicus gave him the opportunity to conquer the Aegean and eastern Mediterranean coasts. The absence of a Persian army provided him with the freedom to concentrate on his role as a liberator to those Greek cities that had fallen under Persian domination. However, although the invasion had got off to a good start, his conquests were far from secure. For the meantime, Alexander had neutralized any substantial threat from the Persians on land. The main concern for Alexander now became the Persian fleet, which was about to enter the Aegean Sea. The sixteen months between victory at the Granicus and the battle of Issus were crucial in determining whether or not the invasion would succeed. Although there were no major battles during this time, the operational manoeuvres and strategic choices made by both sides would be decisive. Mistakes would be made and opportunities lost on both sides during this period. The end result of these events was the battle of Issus, in which the two great kings would face each other across the battlefield for the first time. The fate of the Persian Empire was about to be decided. This period illustrates effectively that although battles often prove decisive, events off the battlefield can prove equally important to the outcome of a campaign. In this sense, it shows the significance of operational and strategic level decisions. This is also a fascinating period to study because it was during this time that Alexander faced one of his most competent opponents. Until his death in June 333, Memnon was in overall command of Persian operations in the west, including those of the fleet.

This period also provides an ideal opportunity to study the interaction between the naval and land forces on both sides. For their part, the Persians did not make effective use of their maritime forces during this period. They seemed to lack a coherent maritime strategy. Similarly, Alexander made some significant mistakes, although in general he made better strategic use of his joint operations (operations which combined land and naval forces). Neither side seemed to have an effective grasp of the role maritime forces could play in this theatre of operations. However, Alexander's overall strategy was more tolerant of mistakes and bad luck than that of his enemy's. This is usually an essential ingredient of any successful strategy. It is often said that the winner of a chess game is the person who makes the second to last mistake. It often seems to be the same in strategy.

Aside from the battle of Issus and the vital operational and strategic level events, this chapter will also deal with two of Alexander's most famous sieges, at Halicarnassus and Tyre. Both of these were significant Persian naval bases. The latter was the more successful and controversial of the two, but both reveal interesting insights into Macedonian siegecraft.

Historians have questioned the value of both sieges to Alexander's overall plans. Again, these two events present us with an opportunity to analyse Alexander's operational and strategic decision making.

Before Alexander had to concern himself with the fortress of Halicarnassus, he had the task of marching down the Aegean coast, liberating Greek cities as he went. In these early days of the campaigns Alexander seemed more aware of the limited military forces at his disposal, as well as the need to establish stability in the areas conquered. Stability on the Aegean coast was achieved by acting as a liberator to the cities under Persian rule, and by treating their populations with a degree of benevolence. The standard procedure was to prevent looting by his army; establish democracy or retain the satrapal system; respect local traditional laws and customs; and either abolish the tribute paid to the previous Persian rulers, or retain it at the current level. Although Bosworth is correct to downplay the genuine nature of these seemingly benevolent acts, from a strategic perspective they achieved their objectives. Evidence of this can be seen at Sardis, the main Persian city in Lydia. The city and its treasury were surrendered without a fight. In addition, Alexander began the training of young Lydian men for service in his army. From Sardis, Alexander led the army down to the city of Ephesus, where again his rule was accepted without a fight.

The Maritime Environment

The campaign was going well for the young Macedonian, but the Persian fleet was a growing menace. Alexander's next target was Miletus, a coastal city that could act as a good base of operations for Persian naval forces. However, on this occasion Alexander's forces would have to fight for their prize. This task was made much easier by the fact that the Greek fleet of 160 triremes reached Miletus three days before the Persian fleet of 400 ships. With Alexander's naval forces occupying the anchorage on the offshore island of Lade, the Persian fleet was in no position to influence events in Miletus, despite its numerical superiority. However, the Persian ships remained menacingly close at a base 15 km (9 miles) to the north. For some reason Parmenion advised that the Greek ships should put to sea and engage their superior foes. Wisely, Alexander chose not to follow this advice. The king not only feared the consequences of the loss of his fleet, he also understood that his land forces would be depleted in their role as marines in a naval battle. Alexander's decision not to engage the Persian fleet was influenced by a famous, if perhaps mythical event. It is recorded that an eagle was spotted on the beach alongside the Greek fleet. For such a superstitious man as Alexander, this was interpreted as a sign from the god Zeus. Alexander declared that because the eagle was seen on land, that is where he would defeat the Persian fleet, not at sea. The strategic idea behind this declaration was a logical assessment of the existing situation. Aware of his naval inferiority, Alexander played to his strengths. Rather than risk his fleet against the well-trained forces of the Persian navy, Alexander would neutralize them by capturing their naval bases with his land forces. A Persian fleet without bases and ports could make little impact on the land campaign in Asia.

An example of how effective such a strategy could be was the operation around Miletus. Whilst Alexander laid siege to the city, a detachment of cavalry and infantry prevented the Persian fleet from landing forces ashore. This operation, in conjunction with the efforts of the Greek fleet to deny access to the harbour, essentially neutralized the substantial Persian fleet from influencing the fate of Miletus. The nineteenth-century maritime strategist Sir Julian Corbett correctly identified that the value of naval forces can only be truly measured in how they affect the situation on land. Since land is where humans and their main resources reside, land is where strategic decisions must be made. The operation at Miletus is a classic example of this truism. Due to a clever use of forces by Alexander, the Persian fleet had no impact on the events on the shore. In fact, because it was unable to land, the Persian fleet ran low of supplies and had to retreat to Samos.

However, despite the success of Alexander's counter-naval operations at Miletus, Alexander's strategy to defeat the Persian fleet has been questioned in some of the historical literature. Bosworth makes a somewhat convincing claim that the rocky coastline in this area made it impossible for Alexander to deny the Persian fleet safe harbour. Thus, should Alexander capture all of the main ports along the coast, the Persian fleet would still be able to land and thereby disrupt Alexander's communications and undermine his conquered territories. Whilst there is an element of logic and truth in Bosworth's assessment, it lacks a degree of strategic logic. Naval forces require much more than just a sheltered beach to operate effectively. Even the basic fleets of this period required a degree of infrastructure to remain operationally effective. Ships need to be supplied and maintained at regular intervals. By capturing the main naval bases along the coast, Alexander would deny these crucial services to the Persian fleet. The conquest of the coastal populations would also deny the Persians access to manpower reserves. Nonetheless, even in such circumstances the Persian fleet could still act as a nuisance to Alexander if used correctly.

With his forces protected from the Persian fleet, Alexander set about capturing the city of Miletus. He had earlier rejected an offer by the Milesian oligarch for Miletus to be treated as an open city with equal access for both Alexander and the Persians. Thus, the city would have to be besieged. Once the Macedonian siege engines were deployed, the defenders were quickly cleared from the wall, and the wall itself was soon breached. The inhabitants sensibly surrendered once their defences had collapsed. For a city that had resisted his rule, Alexander treated Miletus surprisingly leniently. The majority of the population was left unharmed, although the forces that had defended the city were massacred. The only exception to this was seen in the fate of 300 Greek mercenaries who had fought particularly fiercely against the Macedonians. In contrast to his treatment of such men at the Granicus, Alexander took these Greeks into his army.

We now reach one of Alexander's most questionable strategic decisions, and one that still divides the historical literature to this day. With the Persian fleet still posing a threat, Alexander sent the bulk of his fleet back to Greece. The vessels that remained were to be used for logistical support. There is disagreement in the literature over what exactly happened to the fleet. Bosworth declares that it was

90

demobilized, whereas Hammond states that it was returned to Greece, but ready for recall. The latter seems more likely. The Persian fleet could potentially launch an invasion of the Greek homeland, so it would seem an act of strategic negligence to disband what little naval forces were available to defend against such an eventuality. The decision to send the fleet home was based on a number of factors. In the first instance, Alexander wanted to shift the cost of maintaining the fleet to the Greek Community. More importantly, Alexander quite rightly understood that he could not defeat the Persian navy in an open battle. In which case, his fleet would prove more useful defending the Hellespont against a Persian invasion. However, retaining the fleet along the Aegean coastline would have also served some useful strategic purposes. It could have helped protect crucial land and supply operations from the Persian fleet, as it had at Miletus. It could also have performed a strategic function described by Corbett as a 'fleet in being'. It is always a challenge finding a useful strategic purpose for an inferior navy. The fleet in being role provides such a purpose. Rather than challenge for naval supremacy, merely by its existence a fleet in being keeps the enemy's naval forces occupied. In theory, in this case the Persian fleet would have to maintain a close watch on Alexander's navy to prevent it from operating along the coastline conducting raiding operations and the like.

So, was Alexander right to send his navy back to Greece? On balance the answer is probably yes. To achieve his longer-term goals Alexander had to focus his resources and efforts on the land campaign. The real threat for the Persians came from Alexander's land forces. Although it

91

was a strong naval power, the Persian Empire could not lose the war at sea. Alexander understood that the success he desired would only come on land by defeating the Persian army and conquering Persian territory. And although operating in Asia without a fleet left him somewhat vulnerable to Persian maritime operations, his conquest of the coastal cities would over time reduce the effectiveness of this threat. Also, if he could achieve victory on land against the Persian army, the naval theatre of operations would become redundant. In the meantime, Alexander had to do what he could to defend Greece from Persian operations. A Persian expedition to the Greek mainland represented the greatest threat from the Persian fleet. However, as if to illustrate what a difficult decision this was, Alexander had to commission a new fleet in 333. Bosworth claims that this supports his criticism of Alexander's decision to send the fleet home. However, it may be more accurate to suggest that in his original decision to send the fleet home Alexander had merely chosen the lesser of two evils. In the following year he made a slightly different assessment of situation.

On balance then, it seems that Alexander made what can be regarded as the correct strategic judgement about the use of his maritime forces. But, what of the Persian navy? Again, judgement concerning Memnon's use of his naval forces is a close call. At one level, the most obvious choice for Memnon would have been to lead an expedition to the Greek homeland as Alexander feared. The objective of such an operation would have been to encourage some of the Greek city-states to rebel once again against Macedonian hegemony. However, at this time Memnon decided to hold Halicarnassus. The decision not to attack Alexander's homeland appears to have been an error by Memnon. After the victory at the Granicus, and the subsequent capture of many significant cites along the coast, the initiative was clearly with Alexander. It is precisely when facing such circumstances that one should attempt to put the enemy off-balance and regain the initiative for oneself. A successful expedition to Greece would have at least diverted Alexander's attention, maybe some of his resources, and ultimately may have required him to return home to deal with the threat. The Roman Republic managed to draw Hannibal away from Italy in 203 when it invaded North Africa and threatened Carthage itself.

However, in Memnon's defence it can be argued that he may simply have been attempting to stem the tide of Alexander's coastal conquests. Alexander's campaign down the Aegean coast had already built up momentum. By holding Halicarnassus Memnon could delay Alexander, and perhaps even inflict a small defeat upon him. A defeat could have significant ramifications on the cities in Alexander's path further down the coast. A military setback would show that the Macedonian was not invincible, and that perception might inspire greater levels of resistance to his conquest. Also, Memnon may have been thinking for the longer-term. Holding Halicarnassus might not prove decisive in the short-term, but it offered the best opportunity to maintain a well-fortified base of operations for later campaigns, including an attack on Greece. The Persian navy needed a safe base of operations; Halicarnassus might have been it. The city was also the home of a substantial Persian weapons store. For the man who had advised against fighting Alexander at the Granicus, the decision to hold Halicarnassus seems in character. However, despite the logic of this decision an expedition to Greece seemed to offer the most promise. Even if Halicarnassus could be retained, Memnon would still have to go on the offensive with the Persian fleet; why not do so now? A small setback in Asia could interrupt Alexander's schedule, but a successful rebellion in Greece could end his campaigns altogether. From Alexander's perspective, Halicarnassus not only represented another objective in his quest to control all of the main naval bases along the Aegean coast, he also understood that it was an ideal point from which his enemies could launch an attack on Greece.

The Siege of Halicarnassus

At Halicarnassus Memnon had gathered Persian troops, part of the Persian fleet and many Greek mercenaries. However, the greatest defensive attribute of the city was its fortifications. It had a surrounding moat 13m (45 ft) wide and 6.5m (22 ft) deep; 1.8m (6 ft) deep walls; high masonry towers; three strong citadels, one of which was on a small island at the entrance to the harbour; and finally a good stock of weapons. In addition, now that the Persians had uncontested command of the sea, the city could be supplied indefinitely through the harbour. It seemed that Memnon was in a strong position. However, a mismanagement of the Persian fleet allowed Alexander's small supply fleet to move the siege engines and supplies from Miletus for the siege of

94

Halicarnassus. Even if we accept the strategic logic of Memnon's decision not to launch an expedition against Greece, there is no excuse for allowing Alexander's remaining vessels to operate with this degree of freedom. The large Persian fleet should have been keeping a close-eye on the Greek ships, and should have taken the opportunity to engage and destroy them at any opportunity. Nonetheless, despite this lapse, Halicarnassus still presented a difficult challenge even for the skilled Macedonian siege engineers.

Alexander first reconnoitred the eastern Mylasa gate. In response, the defending forces revealed their intention to resist by launching an aggressive sortie which disrupted Alexander's preparations. The Macedonian then moved to the western side of the city. Finally, Alexander began the siege in earnest by filling-in a section of the moat at the northern wall. This enabled him to deploy his siege towers and rams, and thus he could begin to weaken the city's defences. Torsion catapults were used to clear defenders from the walls, whilst the walls themselves were slowly weakened. The Macedonians' progress was interrupted by a series of sorties and attacks from within the city. Siege towers were burned, and some of the besiegers killed. In one notable incident, 16 Macedonians were killed and 300 were wounded. However, despite these setbacks the defences were eventually breached. The Persians responded by building a second, crescent-shaped defensive wall to cover the breach in the outer wall. From this, the Persians were able to rain down missile fire on the Macedonians. Alexander was making progress, but it was slow and costly. At one stage he even had to parley with the defenders to be able to recover his dead. Bosworth reminds us that this was a unique event in Alexander's campaigns. Despite the fierce resistance, Alexander was on the verge of breaching the second defensive wall.

With defeat imminent, Memnon and his generals decided to launch one last assault against their attackers. Whilst covering fire was supplied from the walls and towers, two groups of 1,000 Greek mercenaries would launch a coordinated attack at night. Two Athenians, Ephialtes and Thrasybulus, would command the attack. One detachment would attack and attempt to burn the siege towers. When the Macedonian troops hopefully responded and went to the defence of the towers, the second detachment of mercenaries would attack the enemy's flank and drive them from the walls inflicting heavy casualties. At first, this surprise attack went well. The Macedonians did exactly as predicted and rushed to defend the towers. At this point, the phalanx of the second unit of Greek mercenaries fell upon the Macedonians' flank and began to drive them back. For a while Memnon must have thought that he might just achieve the victory he so desired over Alexander. However, the Macedonian forces that had been surprised, and were now under severe pressure, were young and relatively inexperienced. The situation was rescued by the arrival of veterans from Philip's days, who stabilized the situation and then began to throw the mercenaries back into the city. Memnon had come close to success, but Alexander's luck prevailed; albeit luck built upon a strong professional army. Memnon had played his last card, and had failed to hold the city wall. Despite this reverse; however, Memnon was not completely defeated. He burned the defences around the wall and retreated with his troops into the well-fortified citadels. After the costly siege of the outer walls, the Macedonians had no will to begin another siege against the citadels. Thus, Alexander left a garrison of 3,000 infantry and 200 cavalry to invest the citadels. However, the remaining Persian troops could be supplied and reinforced by the Persian navy. In essence, Alexander had failed to remove the Persian military presence from Halicarnassus, and had left them with a base of operations. It was a failure that nearly cost him dearly in the following year.

Before embarking on the next stage of the campaign, Alexander allowed the recently married amongst his troops to return to their families for the winter season. This won him a great deal of support amongst his men, and also enabled the escorting officers to raise fresh recruits for the coming year. With the costly siege of Halicarnassus behind him, Alexander now continued with the conquest of the coastal region. However, the territories he controlled on the coast were vulnerable to attack from the hinterland. Enemy forces had easy access to this part of the coastal region through a series of river valleys. This problem was intensified by Alexander's perennial problem of a shortage of forces. He simply did not have enough men to guard all of these access points. In true Alexander fashion he would solve the problem by going on the offensive. However, in order to achieve this, and at the same time continue his conquest of the coastal region, Alexander would have to divide his forces. This is an example of how important it is for a commander to have trusted generals he can rely upon. On this, as on so many other occasions, Alexander was able to rely upon Parmenion. In this instance Parmenion was given the task of conquering the Anatolian plateau. The two halves of the army would reunite at Gordium the following spring.

Again, Alexander's conquest of the coast required little serious fighting for the most part. One of the most serious clashes occurred against the Pisidians as Alexander was heading north from the coast to meet with Parmenion at Gordium. The clash occurred outside the city of Sagalassus, where local fighters held a steep hill. Alexander led a frontal attack of 7,500 phalangites, with archers and Agrianians protecting the right flank, and Thracian javelin-men on the left flank. In the assault Alexander lost twenty men, many of them archers, but his heavy infantry was far too strong for the light-armed Sagalassians. The enemy lost 500 killed, and the city was taken. As planned, the army was eventually reunited at Gordium in April 333. This included the arrival of the new recruits and married men from Macedonia. Since Halicarnassus, Alexander had made more striking progress. However, one of his worse fears was about to materialize.

As Alexander was heading to Gordium, Memnon had finally taken the decision in March 333 to launch an expedition to Greece. At last, Persia's maritime power was about to be put to good use. One of the key characteristics of maritime power is the flexibility it gives to overall strategy. In this instance, it allowed Persia to shift the geographic focus of the campaign and attempt to seize the initiative back from Alexander. Up until this point, for the most part Alexander had been dictating the course of the war. Memnon was now sailing into the Aegean with 300 triremes, Greek mercenaries, and a large quantity of money. Memnon took the islands of Chios and Lesbos quickly. The only real resistance on Lesbos occurred at Mytilene, where mercenaries sent by Alexander managed to hold back the Persian forces, and compel the invaders to besiege the city. These events clearly worried Alexander, who commissioned a new fleet at enormous cost to repel the invaders. The League of Corinth was also required to provide naval forces under its treaty obligations. Thankfully for the Macedonian king, the Greek states remained loyal. More importantly, Memnon's entire expedition was undermined by a decision by Darius. In an act of strategic schizophrenia, in the middle of a successful maritime expedition Darius shifted the focus back to the land where he intended to defeat Alexander in a great land battle. For this, Darius recalled large sections of his forces from the west. This order stripped perhaps 200 ships from the expeditionary forces besieging Mytilene. To make matters worse, Memnon died of an illness during the siege. Even though Mytilene eventually fell to the Persians and a number of gains were made in the Hellespont, stripped of resources the maritime operations in the Aegean were fatally under-mined. Just as the Persians had begun to wrestle the initiative from the Macedonians, Darius had played right into Alexander's hands. The fate of the campaign would now rest on a pitched land battle, which was just the sort of situation in which Alexander excelled.

The Battle of Issus

Darius now began raising a new army at Babylon for the coming showdown with Alexander. It soon became clear to Alexander that Darius was on the march west to the Syrian coast. At this stage Alexander's dominant strategic concern was to prevent joint operations between the Persian fleet and army. In particular, he feared that the fleet could be used to land the army in his rear and thereby cut his communications to Greece. To counter this threat, Alexander took the rational, if somewhat risky decision to divide his forces. He ordered Parmenion to clear the coast of Persian satrapal forces, down to the Pillar of Jonah. For this task Alexander gave him a force composed of the Thessalian cavalry, Greek and Balkan infantry, and some Greek mercenaries. Alexander led the rest of the army inland into Cilicia to engage Darius' army before it could unite with the fleet. However, Darius outmanoeuvred Alexander. The Macedonian thought that Darius was at Sochoi, and therefore was not in his rear. In fact, after a march of three months from Babylon, and a flanking manoeuvre to the north, the Persian army had managed to reach the coast north of Alexander and had cut his land communications with Greece without the aid of the Persian fleet. However, luck had not abandoned the Macedonian. By sheer chance, Alexander had just reunited his forces with Parmenion's troops. Had Darius arrived in the vicinity twenty-four hours earlier, he could well have been positioned between Alexander's two armies. This would have given the Persian ruler the advantage of interior lines of communication and the opportunity to defeat each of the enemy armies in turn. Nevertheless, Alexander still faced the problem of having the enemy in his rear. To add insult to injury, when Darius arrived at Issus he killed the sick and wounded left there by Alexander. The two great generals were now within striking distance of each other: but who would take the initiative?

When and where the battle would be fought was heavily influenced by the size of the respective armies, the supply situation, and the psychology of the two opposing commanders. There is a lack of consensus in the sources concerning the exact size of Darius' army. However, there is agreement on the fact that at Issus, Alexander faced a Persian army significantly larger than his own. The Macedonian ruler had under his command 26,000 infantry and 5,300 cavalry. With an advantage in numbers Darius would prefer to fight on the open plains; whereas Alexander sought to negate his enemy's numerical advantage by waging battle in the coastal narrows. However, Darius could not wait for long. With the harvest long over, Darius' large army could not sustain itself indefinitely. Just as significant was the psychology of the situation. As a proud, divine ruler Darius was compelled to seize the initiative against an inferior force. This was fuelled by Alexander's clever statesmanship. In order to goad Darius, Alexander conducted athletic events as a sign of his contempt for the great Persian ruler. As a result of these moves Darius ordered his army south into the coastal narrows.

The Persian forces marched south from Issus and took up a strong defensive position on the bank of the river Payas. This mountain stream, sourced from the Amanus mountain range, was easily fordable. Nonetheless, it provided some form of obstacle that might disrupt the mighty Macedonian phalanx, upon which Alexander's tactics would again be based. However, this potential advantage was in many respects negated by the narrow dimensions of the battle-field. At only 2.4 km (1.5 miles) in width from the foot of the mountains to the sea, the site of battle would severely

101

negate Darius' numerical advantage. In contrast to the situation at Granicus, on this occasion the Persians deployed their best infantry along the riverbank in a strong defensive position. In the centre of his line Darius placed his Greek mercenaries. In fact, at Issus Darius had the greatest number of Greek mercenaries ever to fight on the side of the Persians. On either side, lightly armed Persian 'Cardaces' and archers flanked these forces. Immediately to the rear of these frontline forces stood Darius and his 3,000 strong Royal Cavalry Guard. Any gaps in this section of the line were filled by stockades. To the rear were placed the Asiatic levies. The forces thus described had a mainly defensive role in the coming battle. Their objective would be to hold and pin the Macedonian forces as they attacked. This would leave the decisive offensive action to be undertaken by the massed cavalry deployed on the Persian right. The objective for these forces was to break through the Macedonian left, and then strike the rest of the line in the flank and rear. There seems to be a great deal to recommend such a plan. Darius clearly had little hope of breaking the mighty Macedonian phalanx in the centre of Alexander's line. It therefore seemed sensible to rest his hopes on the Persians' most reliable forces, the cavalry, and attack the Macedonian flank.

Against this plan, Parmenion's forces on the left would once again play a crucial role. It took most of the morning for Alexander's forces to move into line. Initially, Alexander had deployed only the Greek cavalry on the extreme left. However, once he noticed the mass of Persian cavalry on that side of the battlefield he ordered the Thessalian cavalry to redeploy, and so reinforced the

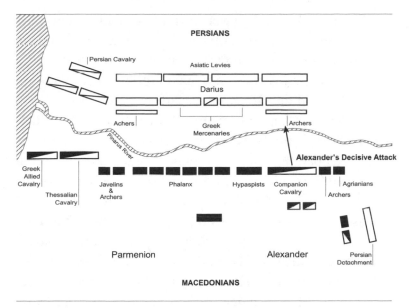

The Battle of Issus

Greeks. Hoping to deceive the Persians of his intentions, Alexander hid the movement of the Thessalian cavalry with the massed ranks of the phalanx. So, at the beginning of the battle the Persian cavalry would have to engage both the Thessalian and Allied Greek cavalry, a force of 2,500, in a mighty clash of cavalry. Also under the command of Parmenion on the left were Thracian javelin men, Cretan archers, and four battalions of phalanx. As at the Granicus, the right of the line was to be the instrument of decision under Alexander's control. These forces consisted of two phalanx battalions; next came two brigades of hypaspists; the Royal Brigade of the Companion cavalry (commanded by Alexander); the remainder of the Companion cavalry; and the line was completed by archers and Agrianians. As the forces deployed for battle, immediately to the rear of

103

the Companion cavalry were the Prodromoi lancers and Paeoian light horse. Finally, to guard against a Persian detachment in the hills on his right, Alexander deployed a squadron of light horse and some Agrianian infantry. In reserve he held the Greek mercenaries.

As the moment of battle drew close, Alexander, obviously still concerned by the Persian detachment on his right, extended the line to the right by transferring two ilai of Companions and some of the reserve Greek mercenaries. In many respects, Alexander's plan was similar to that of Darius. He intended Parmenion's forces on the left to hold back the Persian cavalry, whilst the Companions would force through the Cardaces and take the Greek mercenaries in the flank and rear. The plan was classic Greek warfare, with a twist of Alexander. As in traditional hoplite battle from the past two centuries, the phalanx of Greek mercenaries would be defeated by creating a gap in the line; breaking through; and then routing the rest of the line by threatening its rear. As both sides faced each other across the river, in what could be the decisive battle of the campaign, Alexander rode along his lines both to inspect his forces and also to hearten the men before the clash of arms. As he rode in front of them, the young king called out the names of his officers and those men in the ranks who had gloried themselves in past actions.

In many respects, Alexander's plan rested on the speed of his advance. He needed to cover the ground between the two forces rapidly. This would minimize the opportunity for the Persian archers to deplete his forces with their arrows. A rapid assault would also allow Alexander to catch some of the Persian forces in mid-manoeuvre. There has been some debate amongst historians concerning the status of the Cardaces. Were they hoplites or peltasts? The evidence would suggest that they were in fact the more lightly armed peltasts, who on occasions did operate with archers to their front. Placing archers in front of infantry in this manner required careful coordination and preparation. Ideally, once the archers had fired a few rounds, the infantry line behind would open to allow the archers to pass through. Clearly this was an operation fraught with risk; the timing had to be just right. If the timing was off, either the archers or infantry would be caught unprepared by the advancing forces.

Alexander, leading the Royal Squadron across the river, launched the attack. Following closely behind were the Companions, the hypaspists, light horse and Agrianians. It seems that the archers in front of the Cardaces were indeed caught in the open and ridden down by Alexander's cavalry. The Cardaces themselves could not stand against the Macedonian assault, and the Persian left began to crumble. All seemed to be going well for the Macedonian king, but the battle of Issus was to be a close-run affair. As already noted, speed would be key to Macedonian victory. However, it also proved on this occasion to be almost the undoing of the legendary Macedonian phalanx. As the forces under Alexander surged forward, the two battalions of phalanx under his command were dragged towards the Persians at a quicker pace than the four battalions under Parmenion, who faced steep banks of the river. The phalanx line split. This was the sort of opportunity that any force facing a Greek or Macedonian phalanx prayed for. Such a split exposed the vulnerable flanks and rear of the phalanx. At the same time that this was occurring, the Persian cavalry was pushing the

Thessalian cavalry backwards. In the centre, the Persian-Greek mercenaries grasped the opportunity presented to them and pushed the disrupted phalanx back, killing 120 Macedonians in the process.

The battle of Issus had reached its moment of decision. If the Macedonian phalanx crumbled, then the foundations upon which Alexander's entire plan was based would be undone. Parmenion's cavalry would be isolated on the left, and the forces attacking the Persians on the right could be struck in their flank and rear. However, at this critical juncture, with his left wing collapsing and Alexander pushing ever closer to him, Darius took the decision to flee the battlefield in his chariot. There has been some debate concerning how long Darius stood his ground. Arrian's account has the Persian ruler fleeing the scene of battle almost as soon as Alexander's attack began to bear fruit. In contrast, some modern scholarship indicates that Darius fought bravely and stood his ground until his own royal guard was destroyed around him and capture seemed imminent. Regardless of how bravely Darius fought, his exit from the battle sealed the fate of his army. With the left and centre of the Persian line now collapsing, Alexander was able to concentrate on saving the phalanx. He ordered the hypaspists and the two battalions of the phalanx that had advanced to wheel to the left and engage the Greek mercenaries in their flank. There is also evidence to suggest that elements of the Macedonian cavalry joined in this mauling of the mercenaries. This gave the four battalions of the phalanx the opportunity to regain their order and push forward against the Greeks. The sight of the Persian forces on the left and in the centre falling back gave renewed confidence to Parmenion's men on Alexander's left, and at the same time sapped the will of the Persian cavalry. In turn, they too took the decision to flee the battlefield.

It is at this point that we can appreciate the advantages to be gained from Alexander's emphasis on the pursuit of defeated enemy forces. In traditional hoplite warfare pursuit and attempted annihilation of the enemy were rarely undertaken. In this more ritualistic form of conflict both sides recognized the outcome reached on the field of battle, and having agreed on appropriate compensation for the victors, the defeated were allowed to return to their homes. Alexander, like his father, had a much more total approach to war. For this, some modern scholars have derided him. He has been accused of brutalizing the art of warfare in ancient Greece. Without question, Alexander was responsible for many acts of brutality against innocent non-combatants. Yet, from a strategic perspective, annihilation of the enemy forces in this form of conquest seems entirely appropriate. Alexander's invasion of the Persian Empire was not a mutually agreed contest between similarly organized city-states with a common code of behaviour. It is unlikely that Darius, with a defeated but largely intact Persian army, would accept Alexander's incursion into his empire for long. In this sense, it made perfect sense to destroy the enemy forces when the opportunity arose. This was also a logical action given Alexander's near term objectives. With the enemy army eradicated as a coherent force, Alexander could concentrate on conquering the Syrian coast. If annihilation of the enemy is your objective, then the pursuit is the best opportunity to achieve that goal. A routed army loses its cohesion as an organized force. Rather than resisting as a whole, it tends to fracture into small, or even individual components. In this particular case, the confusion and casualties were intensified by the fact that the heavy cavalry was the last to leave the battlefield. As this force fled, it would have ploughed into the slower-moving Persian infantry. As it was, although heavy losses were inflicted on the fleeing Persian army, they were saved from absolute annihilation by the coming darkness. Nonetheless, as a functioning force Alexander had destroyed Darius' Grand Army. As an added bonus, Alexander had also captured members of the Persian royal family, including Darius' wife and mother. These royal prisoners were given their due respect, and in general were very well treated by Alexander.

Issus: The Assessment

Although outnumbered and facing the Persian ruler himself across the field of battle, Alexander had again achieved a decisive victory. How had this occurred? In contrast to the battle of the Granicus, at Issus the Persians had much in their favour. Again, the Macedonian king had to attack across a stream. However, on this occasion the Persians had correctly placed their infantry in the front line. This allowed Darius to concentrate his cavalry forces on the right, and thereby attempt a decisive outflanking manoeuvre. However, a number of factors ensured that this reasonably solid plan would fail. Firstly, because of Alexander's goading and for logistical reasons, Darius had foregone the advantages of fighting on wide-open plains.

The narrow coastal landscape negated his numerical advantage and severely lessened his chances of outflanking his foe. Perhaps of more importance than this was the inferiority of much of Darius' infantry. Aside from the Greek mercenaries, the Persian infantry could simply not stand in the face of Alexander's cavalry assault. Again, the inferiority of the Persian infantry javelin in the face of Macedonian lances and sarissae was a significant factor in the outcome. Without a secure base of infantry, the excellent Persian cavalry would be isolated and vulnerable. Finally, we must look to Alexander himself. As in previous campaigns in the Balkans, the speed of his assault, focused as it was on a weak point in the enemy line, made it almost impossible for the enemy to adapt to the rapidly deteriorating situation. For sure, the speed of attack at Issus was too rapid for the Macedonian phalanx. The splitting of the phalanx on this occasion throws up some questions regarding Alexander's pre-battle planning. Why were the four battalions of the phalanx left behind by this rapid engagement of the enemy? Nevertheless, the same mind that had perhaps overlooked this possibility also managed to recognize the impending crisis and rectify it with the redeployment of his forces mid-battle. Alexander's *coup d'oeil* was again evident.

The Siege of Tyre

Following his victory at Issus, Alexander had essentially two choices; he could pursue Darius back into Persia, or he could continue on his quest to capture the coastal ports. Alexander

109

chose the latter. His objective now was the conquest of Phoenicia: a region that has been described as a land of city-states. Many of these city-states, such as Sidon and Byblus, submitted to Alexander's rule without a contest. However, this part of the campaign was not to be without a bloody and lengthy contest. One of the most significant ports in Phoenicia was the island-city of Tyre. Indeed, Tyre was the dominant sea power in Phoenicia. Initially, it seemed that Alexander would be able to add this prize to his conquests without a struggle. The Tyrians essentially accepted Alexander's hegemony in the region, but declared their ultimate neutrality by forbidding either Persians or Macedonians to enter the city. This declaration of neutrality was in response to Alexander's demand to make a sacrifice to Heracles in the state temple. An impasse had been reached; Alexander decided to end it by laying siege to the city. There has been considerable debate about both the motivations and strategic rationale in the decision to besiege Tyre. For some writers the decision seemed to be motivated by the impetuous temper of the young king. It is argued that Alexander could simply have left a garrison on the mainland to watch over this important city until it came to its senses and capitulated to his demands. However, there were two main strategic motivations for engaging in the siege. Firstly, if the Persian fleet had access to ports such as Tyre it could continue to threaten Alexander's communications back to Greece. The further Alexander ventured into the Persian Empire, the more important it was to have secure lines of communication back home. It would seem that a land-based garrison could not neutralize the functioning of a port such as Tyre. The city could continue to function through sea-based communications. Indeed, there is some evidence to indicate that Tyre had received promises of aid from Carthage. Secondly, the young king recognized the importance of deterrence. An aggressive and successful response to the Tyrians' resistance would send a clear message to any other cities in his path that had similar thoughts. A successful policy of deterrence requires capability, commitment and communication. To be deterred, any potential future adversaries need to be convinced that you have the capability and will to inflict significant punishment upon them should they transgress. This ability to punish has to be communicated to those who need deterring. What better way to communicate such a threat than to actually enact it against the unfortunate Tyrians?

Tyre, with a population of approximately 40,000, was built upon an islet 800m (0.5 mile) from the mainland. As the siege began in January 332 Tyre was well fortified (with walls 45m (150 ft) high on its eastern side), and due to the absence of Alexander's fleet it seemed impregnable. The famous Macedonian siege techniques would be well tested on this occasion. How could Alexander lay close siege to an island fortress? As so often was the case with Alexander, the answer was simple yet ingenious. Under the direction of his chief engineer, Diades, a mole was constructed to connect the city to the mainland, and thereby enable the Macedonian siege engines and forces to begin the arduous task of breaking Tyre. As construction of the mole neared the city walls, the workers became vulnerable to attacks from both the city and Tyrian galleys at sea. In defence, the Macedonians constructed two wooden towers, each 45m (150 ft) high, which protected the workers from attack and were also used as platforms from which catapults could launch projectiles against the city and

111

galleys. However, the Tyrians were well versed in the art of engineering and counterattacked the towers. They constructed a fire ship and sailed it into the mole. So that they could ensure the destruction of the two siege towers, the Tyrians weighed down the back of the ship so that the prow would reach onto the mole and set fire to the towers. This was not the end of their ingenious response. To prevent the Macedonians from quenching the fires they sent troops with the fire ship, who, having abandoned the ship to swim to safety, could now attack and pin down the Macedonians. Finally, other Tyrians landed on the mole and destroyed any other siege engine not engulfed by the fire. Clearly, the siege of Tyre was becoming a fine example of the action-reaction dynamic in warfare. War is conducted against intelligent foes. Therefore, it is essential that commanders consider the potential actions of the enemy, as well as contingency plans to deal with a range of different eventualities. This may seem to be a startlingly obvious statement. However, history is replete with examples of when military commanders have failed to take enough account of the enemy's actions.

The destruction of the siege towers had revealed the significance of local sea control. All the time that the Tyrians had such control they had a degree of flexibility that would enable them to launch counterattacks against the besieging forces. Having thus far concentrated on the land campaign, Alexander now realized that he needed sea power to achieve control of the sea around Tyre. Alexander achieved this goal by slowly gathering elements of the Phoenician fleet to his cause. The rulers of cities such as Sidon and Byblus began to return from sea with their fleets. On arrival they accepted the new political reality, and gave their galleys over to

Alexander. The Macedonians' growing naval strength in the eastern Mediterranean received a significant boost with the addition of 120 galleys from the kings of Cyprus. Their decision seems to have been based on a reading of the political reality after Darius' defeat at Issus. The strategic map of the region was changing, and they were eager to fight on the side of the rising power. As envisaged by Alexander, his victories on the coast were beginning to pay significant dividends at sea. As the coastal ports fell to his armies, the rulers of the Phoenician fleet were compelled to hand over their fleets to the young Macedonian king.

Alexander, along with most of the Cyprian and Phoenician kings, now took his new fleet out to sea. Having initially sought a decisive naval battle, when the Tyrians realized the size of Alexander's fleet they retreated into their two harbours. Alexander now began to blockade them. In many respects, Alexander had already achieved his main objective at sea. When faced with a maritime power such as the Tyrians, one must somehow deny it the ability to exercise its naval power. Of course, the ideal solution would be to defeat their fleet in a decisive naval engagement. However, failing that, the next best course of action is to use a strategy of 'sea denial'. By blockading their fleet in harbour, Alexander was doing precisely that. He had denied the Tyrians effective use of their sea power assets. This had two main effects. Firstly, they could no longer molest his besieging forces operating on the mole. Secondly, the blockade would prevent supplies reaching the besieged population within the city.

Now that Alexander had Tyre besieged from both the sea and land he could build more siege engines, knowing they were safe from destruction. In this vein, he had new siege towers, catapults and rams constructed. There is some evidence that some of the rams were deployed on naval vessels. Fuller speculates that this enabled Alexander to assault the city walls from a number of positions, rather than just from the mole. Although the tide had shifted in favour of the Macedonians, the Tyrians were still putting up a substantial fight. On the battlements overlooking the mole the Tyrians had constructed wooden towers and catapults. It is also reported that they harried Alexander's ram-ships with the use of fire-arrows. Finally, large stone blocks had been sunk at the foot of the walls around the mole to obstruct anchorage of the ram-ships. However, these stones were slowly dragged clear and removed by cranes. Once this obstacle had been overcome, the Tyrians continued in their efforts to foil the ram-ships. They did this by breaking the blockade with armoured ships and using divers to cut the anchor ropes that were holding the ram-ships in place. Alexander responded with his own armoured ships and by replacing the anchor ropes with chains.

Although Alexander had seemingly overcome the best efforts of the Tyrians to break the siege, they were about to deliver one last surprise. It has already been noted that luck often played a part in Alexander's victories (his rescue by Cleitus at the Granicus being perhaps the most obvious to date), and so it was at Tyre. Taking advantage of the fact that Alexander and the Cyprian crews retired to the shore each day for lunch, the Tyrians deceived the enemy of their intentions and launched a surprise raid with ten of their finest ships. Thankfully for Alexander, on this occasion he had not taken his usual afternoon siesta. Consequently, he was able to rally his forces and mount a counterattack. The Tyrian assault was thrown back, with the loss of only four Cyprian quinquiremes. Alexander's predictable routine suggested a degree of complacency on his part, and had nearly cost him dear. Fuller suggests that had a more sizable Tyrian force been sent out, Alexander's forces could have dealt a serious blow. As it was, the Macedonian's quick reaction and leadership had limited the damage.

The siege was proving to be increasingly costly and lengthy. Alexander therefore made a concerted effort to find a weak spot in the enemy's defences. He found such a point in the wall just south of the Egyptian Harbour. Here the wall was assaulted and breached before the attackers were thrown back by dogged resistance. However, Alexander now focussed his efforts on this breach. His forces would attempt to enlarge the breach, and thus compel the Tyrians to concentrate their forces in that area. At that moment Alexander would throw his enemy into confusion by launching assaults into the two harbours, and attack various other sections of the walls with catapults and archers from galleys. Alexander was attempting to deceive and then overwhelm the defenders.

The attack on the breach commenced. Initially, ram-ships led the assault in order to enlarge the breach. Once this was achieved, Admetus' hypaspists and Coenus' battalion of phalanx, under the command of Alexander, took up the attack. Admetus led his men in the first wave of the assault. They managed to capture a section of the wall that flanked the breach. During the attack Admetus was felled by a spear. Nonetheless, the hypaspists had done their job, and Alexander led the phalanx into the breach. In bitter fighting, the Macedonians pushed through the defences and on towards the royal palace. Alexander's plan was going well. At the same time that his forces were forging into the city through the breach, his naval vessels had broken into the two harbours and had landed men in the city. Eventually, the Tyrians fell back on the Shrine of Agenor to make their last stand. Alexander now led the hypaspists in the final attack. Once the fighting had transferred into the city, there was no real contest. The professional and well-armed men under Alexander soon defeated any coordinated resistance that remained.

A siege that had initially seemed avoidable had lasted seven months and become increasingly hard fought. As a signal to those in the future who might consider resisting Alexander's hegemony, and perhaps in an act of rage, the Macedonian king treated the populace of Tyre with brutality. An estimated 8,000 Tyrians were killed, and the other 30,000 were sold into slavery. However, amnesty was granted to a few important Tyrians, including King Azemilk, and those who had sought sanctuary in the temple of Heracles. For the purposes of this study, Tyre is perhaps the best example of Macedonian siege technique during the campaigns. It is also a classic example of the dynamic interplay between belligerents. In many respects, the Tyrians presented Alexander with some of his most competent enemies. The Tyrians' countermeasures to the Macedonian siege are worthy of our praise. However, although Alexander suffered a number of setbacks during the siege, the operations around Tyre further enhance his reputation as a military commander. Particularly noteworthy is Alexander's appreciation of the joint environment in this context. He came to understand the significance of local sea control. Once this had been achieved, Alexander could fully display his tactical ingenuity. The final assault on the city from a number of directions, utilizing both land and sea forces, is an outstanding example of joint operations. As in his land battles, Alexander understood that by coordinating the efforts of different units he could multiply the military effect of the overall force.

4

The Battle of Gaugamela and
The Fall of the Persian Empire

After the great victory at Issus and the costly, but successful siege of Tyre, Alexander must have hoped that his march down the remainder of the Mediterranean coast would be relatively peaceful. Although for the most part this was true, just along the coast from Tyre, Alexander's forces would have to engage in another lengthy siege at Gaza. Again, this event would test the Macedonian siege technique and once again display the ruthlessness of Alexander's response to resistance. Beyond Gaza lay Egypt, the western-most satrapy of the Persian Empire. Although Alexander's capture of Egypt was a peaceful affair, his period in the satrapy witnessed some significant events in the young king's life. These events would have great influence on Alexander, and therefore also on his future campaigns more generally. In many respects though, this period represented the calm before the storm. For, whilst Alexander was in Egypt, Darius was planning his next move. The Persian ruler was making both diplomatic

119

and military preparations to save his empire. These efforts would eventually lead to the final great battle between the two rulers at Gaugamela, ten months after the rout of Darius' army at Issus. In some important ways Gaugamela was a very different battle to that at Issus. Although Alexander was outnumbered once again, on this occasion his enemy would choose the site of battle so as to maximize his numerical superiority. Gaugamela would be a close-run affair, but again Alexander achieved a decisive victory. How he achieved this is revealing in terms of how the different factors that comprise victory combine together. Finally, this chapter will deal with the operations in the immediate aftermath of Gaugamela, during which Alexander's operational art and outstanding manoeuvres ensured the capture of the Persian capitals, and thereby brought the war with Persia to a close.

The Siege of Gaza

Gaza lay 241km (150 miles) to the south of Tyre. The city was a significant strategic objective. To bypass the city would be to leave a Persian stronghold on Alexander's lines of communication. This would have implications from a physical security perspective as well as having political and strategic effects. From a security angle, Alexander would have to leave forces investing Gaza, as he had done at Halicarnassus. Troops would have to be left to prevent Persian forces conducting operations to disrupt Alexander's rule in the area. This would further deplete the forces available to him. Leaving Gaza in Persian hands could also undermine the reputation of Alexander amongst the local population. For Alexander, hegemony was the only option. The king understood the need to neutralize any alternative centres of authority. Local populations must not be left with any choices with regards to the centres of power that they would obey. So, Alexander would attempt to take the city. However, the governor of the city, Batis, had prepared for Alexander's arrival. The city was fortified and stood atop a mound 76m (250 ft) high, which in turn was protected by a high wall. Batis had hired Arab mercenaries to defend the city, and had stockpiled supplies to withstand the inevitable siege. Working on the ambitious and risky assumption that Alexander's forces would not be able to breach the city's defences, Batis refused the Macedonian's demands for surrender.

However, Gaza did pose Alexander's siege engineers a serious challenge. The mound prevented the Macedonians from deploying their siege engines close to the city walls. This was a significant obstacle to the well-established Macedonian siege technique. When advised of this by his men, Alexander's response is yet another instance in which he reveals an acute understanding of the coercive nature of the use of military force. The king realized the future coercive value of taking seemingly impregnable fortresses. This was a strategy that Alexander would use successfully throughout his campaigns. It would also become a characteristic of Roman strategy. Future enemies had to realize that resistance, no matter how well prepared, was futile. The siege engines arrived at Gaza having been moved by sea from Tyre. By this time the Persian navy had ceased to function as an effective force. Thus, once again Alexander

121

was able to use his limited naval forces effectively in support of his land operations.

For the challenge posed by the mound on which Gaza stood, Alexander had a very direct solution. Again, we will see later that Alexander often took a route so direct in his operations that it unbalanced the enemy. Alexander's response to the mound was to build a substantial ramp against the wall, and thus deploy the siege engines on the top. Whilst Alexander's forces constructed the ramp, Batis did not simply look on impassively. He launched a sortie against the workers. In response, Alexander led the hypaspists in a counterattack. In the attack Alexander was struck by a catapult bolt with such force that it pierced his shield and armour and seriously wounded him in the shoulder. As illustrated at the Granicus, in his style of command Alexander always walked a fine line between inspiring his men by example, and recklessly risking the entire campaign should he be killed. Once the ramp was completed, the battering rams and catapults did their job and breached the wall. However, the breach could not be fully exploited, and so the Macedonians also mined the foundations of the wall. As the Macedonians sought to exploit these various breaches, the defenders of the city made valiant attempts to throw the attackers back. Indeed, three attacks were repulsed, until finally another breach had to be made and the walls were scaled in this new area with ladders. Once inside the outer defences, the men of the phalanx who had led the assault managed to throw open the gates of the city, and thereby seal the fate of its defenders. The use of the phalangites in these siege operations demonstrates how flexible a unit they were. Although their primary role was as a heavy, cohesive infantry formation, they were clearly also capable of engaging in urban warfare. Such operations call for a more flexible and mobile form of fighting, and so we can assume that on these occasions the phalangites would have been more lightly armed. The defenders of the city, who had bravely thrown back the Macedonians on three occasions, were all eventually killed in the fighting that ensued. In now familiar fashion, the women and children of the city were sold into slavery.

Some accounts indicate that Batis was singled out for a particularly gruesome end. It is claimed that after having his heels pierced, he was then dragged to his death behind a chariot. The historical accuracy of this account is difficult to prove. Arrian does not mention it at all. If we examine the possible rationale behind such an act we might be able to better judge the likelihood of whether or not it occurred. On a number of future occasions Alexander would prove that leaders who resisted him bravely could sometimes expect lenient treatment, if it suited a strategic purpose. However, to counterbalance this, we have already witnessed how ruthless and brutal Alexander could be to defeated foes at both Tyre and the Granicus. From a strategic perspective, making an example of Batis in such a way could have the effect of deterring any future resistance leaders. It may also be the case that after the long and costly siege of Tyre, Alexander simply did not expect another lengthy siege so soon. Therefore, the king may simply have been angered by Batis' affront to his power. Add to this the fact that Alexander was badly wounded during the siege, and it is not implausible that he vented his anger in such a brutal fashion. In the end, we simply cannot determine the historical accuracy of the accounts of Batis' death. However, such an act is certainly not beyond Alexander, and indeed may have served a logical strategic purpose.

It had taken Alexander two months to take Gaza. The city was repopulated and established as a Macedonian fortress. Although the siege had delayed Alexander for two months and left him with a shoulder injury, the route to Egypt was now under Macedonian control. As at Tyre and the building of the mole, Alexander's engineers at Gaza had proved themselves the equal of a daunting physical task. This task was made more challenging by the local environment. The sandy terrain provided scarce resources for a besieging army. In particular, water would have been difficult to come by in sufficient amounts. Engels estimates that the besieging army would have required over 27 million litres (6 million gallons) of water over the two-month period of the siege. Upon closer analysis it becomes clear just how vital the navy had become for supplying Alexander's campaign along the coast. This only serves to underline the earlier criticism made about the poor maritime-strategy of the Persians. They simply did not understand the strategic value of maritime forces in this war. Alongside the naval forces, the siege engineers must also be regarded as the unsung heroes of the campaigns. Without the skill, innovation and determination of those involved in the siege operations, Alexander's campaigns would have ground to a halt on a number of occasions, or at least would have been far more costly and lengthy. And, as we will see in the next chapter, the Macedonian siege technique would become even more prominent during operations in Afghanistan and India. For now, the fall of Gaza had at last opened the road to Egypt.

The Conquest of Egypt

It was now December 332, and Egypt was seven days hard marching away. Before Alexander set off on his march from Gaza, he sent Amyntas on a recruiting mission to Macedonia. As already noted, Alexander had begun the invasion with a relatively small force. Clever grand strategy and rapid decisive battlefield victories enabled him to conquer and control vast swathes of territory without the need for a massive army. However, the three great sieges at Halicarnassus, Tyre and Gaza had taken their toll on an army that had also waged two large battles against the Persian military. With Darius still in possession of significant manpower resources, and the prospect of encountering increasing resistance the further he ventured into Persia, it was clear that Alexander would require reinforcements. Thankfully, the army would not have to fight for Egypt. Whilst still at Gaza it seems that there must have been advanced negotiations between Alexander and the Persian Satrap of Egypt. The latter surrendered the satrapy, along with its treasury, at Memphis. Indeed, rather than have to fight for Egypt, Alexander was welcomed as a liberator by the Egyptians.

The conquest of Egypt was motivated by a number of factors. Politically and psychologically its capture represented the final act in the conquest of the western part of the Persian Empire. Hammond notes that the capture of Egypt also gave Alexander the opportunity to secure important sea communications that encompassed the entire Aegean and eastern Mediterranean coastlines. These would help stimulate economic interaction in the region. In particular, Egypt was a large producer of grain. Gaining control of this resource would enable Alexander to import grain back to Greece: a net importer of this staple food. There were undoubtedly personal and symbolic reasons as well. The Egyptians proclaimed Alexander Pharaoh, Son of Ra. He also took the opportunity to follow in the footsteps of his ancestors Perseus and Heracles and trekked across the desert to visit the shrine of Zeus Ammon at Siwa. Whilst there he consulted the oracle, and was addressed as Son of God by the attendant priests. This may have increased Alexander's own sense of divinity, which in itself would have negative effects later on in the campaign. Alexander increasingly seemed to believe his own propaganda. This increasing belief in his own divinity would later begin to alienate him from the Macedonian core of the army. Finally, in January 331 Alexander also founded the most famous of his cities, Alexandria. The establishment of cities played a crucial role in the Macedonian king's overall grand strategy. They were designed to be centres of education, trade, and politico-social life. In this respect, the cities would act as an important means for stability and growth in the new empire, and would also engender the process of Hellenisation. In all, Alexander's army spent four months in Egypt.

The Battle of Gaugamela

Having left Egypt, Alexander's forces spent the next few
months building up supplies and mopping up resistance in
Phoenicia and Syria. However, following his defeat at Issus
it seemed that Darius had lost the stomach for another clash
of arms. Having failed on the battlefield, the Persian ruler
now attempted to save his empire through diplomatic
channels. In the summer of 331 he offered Alexander a
treaty of friendship. In return for the safe handover of his
family, Darius offered Alexander all of the territory west of
the Euphrates and 30,000 talents. Parmenion advised
Alexander to accept this offer. However, this advice fell on
deaf ears. The Macedonian king was a young man
brimming with confidence, and with goals that stretched
much further than just the conquest of the western portions
of the Persian Empire. Because of this, it is unlikely that
Darius could ever have diverted Alexander away from his
chosen methods and goals. As it was, in the aftermath of
two decisive military defeats, Darius' offer came far too
late. Thus, Alexander began his march into the heart of his
enemy's territory, seeking a final decisive clash of arms.
Should Alexander have accepted the offer from Darius?

Although Alexander had twice defeated Darius' forces,
this gave him no guarantee that he would succeed again in
battle. Although a well-trained professional army, in the
hands of an excellent tactician, drastically helps to
minimize the chances of defeat, war is always something of
a gamble. The uncertainties in war, many of which come
from the fact that war is a human activity, produce a degree
of unpredictability in the outcome. Taking this truism into

127

account may lead us to criticize Alexander's decision to continue the war. However, there were also dangers in accepting Darius' offer. Leaving Darius in power may simply have given the Persian ruler the time he required to slowly undermine Alexander's position. As it stood, Alexander clearly had the upper hand. His enemy was obviously demoralized, and Alexander had the instrument at his disposal to put an end to Darius' rule. In these circumstances, Alexander made the correct strategic decision to maintain the momentum of the invasion. Military campaigns eventually reach what Clausewitz described as 'the culminating point of victory'. This is the point at which a military overstretches itself and begins to incur diminishing returns on its efforts. Alexander's campaign had not yet reached that point. However, that point would come at a later date.

Whilst Alexander was preparing for the final showdown, Darius was busy mustering a large army at Babylon. This time the forces were drawn from the east and northeast of the empire. Particularly worthy of note were the cavalry from Bactria and Sogdiana. These forces have been described as being on a par with Alexander's Companions. In terms of quantity, this newly raised army was greater than that which had fought at Issus. Exact figures for Darius' army are difficult to come by. The historical sources vary widely in their estimates. The most realistic accounts number Darius' army at Gaugamela as being 250,000 in strength. This was approximately five times as large as Alexander's army at this final battle. Having received intelligence that Alexander was moving through Mesopotamia, Darius moved his vast army north from Babylon into Assyria. Having fought on his

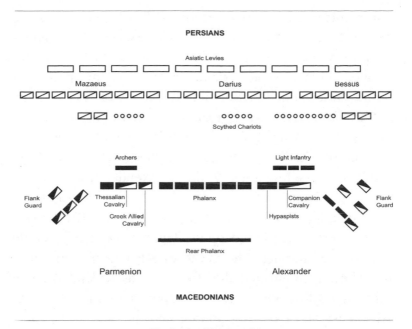

The Battle of Gaugamela

enemy's chosen battlefield at Issus, on this occasion Darius would choose the site of battle. He chose a flat, open plain near the small village of Gaugamela in the Tigris Valley. Since his army was again focused around the cavalry and superior in numbers, Darius chose and prepared a site that was flat and wide. However, he was not entirely satisfied with the terrain that nature had provided, and so the battlefield was levelled-off even further. This levelling would aid both his cavalry and his new striking force of 200 scythed chariots. As well as having scythes projecting from the hubs of their wheels, these chariots were also armed with a heavy spear-headed pole in front.

Also in Darius' favour on this occasion was the fact that Alexander was increasingly stretching his lines of

129

communication, at the same time as Darius was operating nearer to his main bases. In this respect, Alexander's advance was becoming an ever-bigger gamble. A number of great invasions have come to grief on this particular point: the Nazi and Napoleonic invasions of Russia stand out as particularly vivid examples. However, as Engels points out, Alexander's route and the pace of his advance ensured that his army could be supplied. Rather than head south down the Euphrates Valley, Alexander headed east to take advantage of the fertile lands of northern Mesopotamia. The army force marched 345km (215 miles) in just fourteen days to reach the Tigris before Darius could oppose the crossing. The speed of Alexander's arrival at the Tigris also ensured that the Persians had insufficient time to destroy the stores of supplies in that area. As Alexander and the army approached the Tigris, they had anticipated that Darius would contest the crossing of the river. However, the Macedonians had chosen to cross much further north than Darius had predicted. Indeed, the Persian ruler was waiting for the young Macedonian at Gaugamela.

Due to the inaction of his enemy, Alexander was able to rest his men for a few days and reconnoitre the disposition of Darius' forces at Gaugamela. The Persian forces were arrayed in two lines. The first line was mainly composed of cavalry, with the important addition of the scythed-chariots, elephants, and intermingled infantry. The centre of the line was commanded by Darius; with his squadron of Kinsmen, the royal Persian Horse Guard; the remaining 2,000 Greek mercenary hoplites; the Indian and Carian cavalry; and Mardian archers. Out in front of these forces were fifty chariots and fifteen elephants. The left of the line

130

was under the command of Bessus (the Satrap of Bactria). Darius' strategy relied heavily on this section of the line, for it would face Alexander and the Companion cavalry. To this end, he deployed a range of cavalry units, including the Bactrian and Persian horsemen, and in front of these, a hundred chariots. The right of the line was again heavily invested with cavalry, and also had fifty scythed-chariots out front. Behind this first line Darius deployed the majority of his infantry. Although large in number, this mass of ethnically diverse levies was neither equipped nor capable of disciplined phalanx warfare against Alexander's well-drilled heavy infantry. Once again, the Persian battle plan rested upon a weak foundation of infantry. Nonetheless, Darius had made some technological progress since his first meeting with Alexander at Issus. His cavalry were no longer armed with the javelin, but instead wielded a longer sword and thrusting-spear. There had been some changes on the defensive front as well. His infantrymen were equipped with a larger shield, and some of his cavalry had link-armour.

Darius' plan was necessarily focused on his cavalry. The aim was to create a situation in which the manoeuvrability and numbers of the cavalry could be brought to bear against the flanks and rear of Alexander's men. It seems that Darius had opted for an offensive plan of operations. By placing his cavalry in the front line on such terrain, he clearly hoped that he could outflank his enemy. The flanking manoeuvre would be aided significantly by the numerical advantage of the Persians, which meant they outflanked the Macedonians by default. The nature of the wide flat terrain of the battlefield would also aid Darius' flanking forces. In contrast to the situation at Issus, on this occasion Alexander did not have the sea and mountains providing natural protection for his flanks. Aside from merely outflanking his opponent on the wings, Darius also hoped to break the cohesion of the phalanx in the centre. This is how the chariots would play their part. The Persian emperor anticipated a frontal assault by Alexander's men. In response, Darius' chariots would charge at the dense formation of the phalanx and break it, thereby creating gaps in the line that the cavalry could exploit. As at Issus, this plan had vulnerabilities, which again centred on the ability of the Persian forces to maintain their cohesion in the face of Alexander's assault. However, unlike the battle of Issus, Darius had a much greater opportunity to allow his cavalry to play the decisive role and outflank the enemy. In this sense, there was a greater chance that Darius could get his decisive blow in first. Quite correctly, Darius understood the need to seize the initiative against Alexander.

Alexander's dispositions at Gaugamela stuck to his tried and tested formula. The whole line, which in comparison to the Persians' was fairly compact and rectangular in shape, was based on the Macedonian phalanx in the centre. To the right of this were the hypaspists, who as usual acted as the linking force between the infantry and cavalry. On their right stood Alexander and the Companion cavalry. In front were Macedonian archers and Agrianian javelin men. Of course, Alexander was perfectly aware of the danger posed by the Persian flanking forces in such an environment. To guard against this threat, on his right he positioned a flank guard consisting of cavalry, javelin men and archers. On the left wing stood the Thessalian and Greek Allied cavalry. Protecting their front were Cretan spearmen and archers. A flank guard made-up entirely of cavalry protected the left flank of the army. As with the flank guard on the right, this force was deployed slightly behind and at an angle to the front line troops. This enabled the guard to face outwards and to the front of the flank they protected. Behind these front line forces, Alexander placed a second line of phalanx infantry made up of Greek mercenaries, Illyrians and Thracians. The main role of this second line of infantry was to turn about to face any Persian attack in the rear. In all, Alexander had under his command 7,000 cavalry and approximately 40,000 infantry. By protecting his flanks and rear, Alexander hoped that the attacking Persian forces could be held at bay whilst the Companions executed their lethal blow. Fuller describes Alexander's plan as defeating an attack of double-envelopment by an attack of penetration.

Initially, Alexander's advance was parallel to the Persian line. However, due to the Persian advantage in numbers, Alexander and the Companions (who were on the right of the Macedonian line) found themselves opposite Darius in the centre of the Persian line. This of course meant that the Persian left seriously overlapped Alexander's right wing. Consequently, as the two lines drew closer, Alexander began to shift his forces to the right. The result of this move was that Alexander's line was now approaching the Persians in an oblique movement. Of course, this now shifted the overlap to Parmenion's troops on the Macedonian left wing. As was the case at Issus, Parmenion would have to hold back the Persian right so as to give Alexander the time he needed to breach the enemy's line.

133

The oblique movement by Alexander now gave him the initiative, and began to threaten Darius' entire plan even before it had been put into effect. As the Macedonian line moved further to the right, there was a danger that the battle would be shifted away from the levelled ground Darius had prepared for his chariots. The Persian ruler had to act quickly before his entire plan unravelled. Darius ordered Bessus to send elements of the Scythian and Bactrian cavalry to assault the Macedonian right flank, and thereby prevent any further movement away from the prepared ground. Alexander responded with a charge by Menidas' mercenary cavalry. There ensued a fierce cavalry engagement, during which the larger Persian force threw Alexander's mercenary cavalry back. The final decisive battle between Alexander and Darius had now begun.

With this first clash of arms tipping in the Persians' favour, Darius perceived that the moment had arrived to throw the scythed-chariots into the fray. His charioteers on the left launched themselves at the right of the Macedonian phalanx. If they were to be successful, they would have to break the cohesion of this central element of the Macedonian line. However, even before they could reach the phalanx, Alexander's light infantrymen began bringing down the horses with volleys of javelins. Those chariots that did reach the main phalanx did little damage. As they approached, the well-drilled phalangites simply opened their ranks to let them pass harmlessly through. Once through the main line, the chariots received their final blow from the grooms of the Companions and the rear ranks of the hypaspists. When one considers the patchy record of scythed-chariots in past battles, it is difficult to understand

134

Darius' faith in them. They had been successfully countered before. Their plight at Gaugamela is a stark reminder of the folly of placing too much faith on one piece of technology or tactic. An enemy as well led and professional as Alexander's army would surely find a way in which to counter such a threat. The hopes vested in the chariots fell like so many of the charioteers and horses as their enemies mauled them.

The sources provide precious few details of what occurred on Parmenion's flank. From the evidence that is available, it seems that the Macedonian left held its ground despite coming under substantial pressure from Persian cavalry forces. The other significant event to occur on that wing of the battle was that Mazaeus (commander of the Persian right) sent a detachment of cavalry to attack the Macedonian base camp. The logic behind such a move is questionable, as the action had no real impact on the course of the battle. There is some suggestion in the sources that this detachment was charged with rescuing Darius' family from the Macedonians. Whilst it seems reasonable that Darius may well have attempted such a rescue, attacking the enemy's rear and base camp could have definite tactical benefits. In particular, sending forces into the enemy's rear may sow panic within their ranks and also seize the initiative by shifting the tactical focus of the enemy. As it was, there is no firm evidence that the royal family was rescued. Similarly, the small scale of the assault ensured that any significant tactical benefits were not realized. This operation was a gesture of wild hope, rather than a well-constructed element of the overall battle plan.

Whilst Parmenion was holding his position against the

Persians on the left, events on the right were reaching the moment of decision. Bessus' forces were still engaged in heavy fighting against Alexander's flank guard. As Alexander committed more of his flank protection forces to this struggle, it seems that Darius also decided to throw increasing numbers of men into this section of the battle. There is some confusion as to why so much of his cavalry were sent to support Bessus, rather than launching an assault against the Companions at the same time. Fuller offers a range of possible explanations. There may have been confusion over the orders; natural impetus may have drawn the reinforcing cavalry to ride to the aid of their fellow horsemen; or the light infantry screen in front of the Companions may have forced the charging cavalry to shift to their left and thereby into Bessus' area of operations. Whatever the cause of this focus on the extreme left of the Persian line, the result could not have been better for Alexander. As the Bactrian cavalry tried to turn the advantage on the left into a decisive engagement, Bessus' forces became increasingly detached from the rest of the Persian line. A gap appeared in the Persian line almost right in front of Alexander and the Companions. Alexander and the Companions now headed a large wedge formation, with the hypaspists and four battalions of the phalanx making up the left side of the wedge, and the right consisting of the Agrianians and infantry flank guard.

In one of the greatest examples of Alexander's tactical technique, the young king, leading the attack, now drove the wedge into the gap. From this point onwards the Persians had lost the day. The force and momentum of a wedge formation headed by heavy cavalry forced the gap in the Persian line to widen quickly. As the Companions broke through the line they now began to strike at the flanks of the Persian front line. With the enemy now at their backs, the day was about to get even worse for these hapless Persians. Just as the reality of their exposed flanks would begin spreading fear and chaos through the Persian forces, the massed ranks of the Macedonian phalanx fell upon them as well. This was classic Alexander: well honed combined-arms tactics in which the enemy was caught between the cavalry and sarissae of the phalanx. With the Persian line now in disarray, Alexander drove his Companions on towards Darius and his entourage. Having failed to capture his adversary at Issus, Alexander was determined to finish the Persian ruler on this day. For Alexander, the personal defeat of the enemy commander would evoke the great heroic tradition of his ancestors. Romantic though he may have been, Alexander was also a great pragmatist and strategist. The slaying or capture of the deified Persian ruler would also symbolize Alexander's personal rise to glory as the new undisputed power in the Persian Empire. Indeed, in the aftermath of the battle Alexander was proclaimed King of Asia.

As the centre of his line began to fail, there came a point when once again Darius took the decision to flee the battle-field. Thus began another of Alexander's tactical hallmarks: the pursuit. As Alexander pushed his forces onwards to chase down his adversary, as at Issus a gap began to develop in the phalanx. The two battalions on the far left of the phalanx stayed in position, and thereby became detached from those battalions who were pushing forward with their king. This gap was exploited by elements of the Persian and Indian cavalry. However, for the Persians this was a case of too little, too late. The enemy forces that had breached the gap were easily dealt with by the rear phalanx who turned and slaughtered the Persians from the rear. This was one of the great ironies for the opponents of Alexander; the moment when his line became disjointed and vulnerable was the same moment at which his own attack had acquired an unstoppable quality. Alexander had seized the initiative, and the speed and momentum of his combined-arms attack ensured that the enemy could never regain control of the battle. This feature of Alexander's tactical prowess also saved both of his flanks at Gaugamela. As the assault in the centre pushed forward, Menidas' flank guard was left isolated in the face of Bessus' superior Bactrian cavalry. Similarly, Parmenion's men were still vastly outnumbered and under heavy assault on the left. However, in both these sectors of the battlefield the Persian forces observed the collapse of the Persian centre and began their own retreat.

One particular event in the battle has caused more discussion than any other, and it concerns whether Alexander broke off his pursuit of Darius to rescue Parmenion's forces on the left flank. The accounts of Plutarch and Arrian both record that Parmenion sent a dispatch rider to seek out Alexander and call upon his aid. In these accounts it is reported that the king shifted the focus of the Companions away from Darius and crossed to the left flank to save Parmenion's men. However, it is likely that these accounts were designed to elevate the heroism of the king, and more importantly to discredit the character of Parmenion. Within the confused, dangerous and dusty environment of the battle, it is unlikely that a messenger could have found and reached Alexander that easily. It seems more plausible that, as mentioned above, the Persian right simply retreated once it had become clear that their centre had collapsed and Darius had left the field of battle. In the event, Alexander pursued Darius without success for 30km (18 miles) until the evening began to draw in. Even though the main action of the battle had long since ended, a final clash of arms resulted in further slaughter of the Persian army. As they returned from the pursuit, the Companion cavalry came across retreating Persian cavalry forces. These Persians, Parthyaeans and Indians had been positioned on the Persian left wing during the battle. The clash that ensued once these two forces met was of great intensity, during which sixty Companions were killed.

It is difficult to estimate with any degree of accuracy the numbers of casualties that fell in the battle. This is primarily because the sources seem unrealistic in their reports of the Persian losses: some quote figures of 250,000. What can be said with certainty is that for the second and decisive time Alexander had defeated the main Persian army. Darius had mustered a huge army for the battle of Gaugamela, and had fought on favourable terrain. Yet, Alexander had not just defeated this army; he had destroyed it as a functioning force. Now, with the reputation and rule of Darius irrevocably damaged, Alexander could invade Babylonia and claim victory over the Persian Empire.

Gaugamela: The Assessment

In attempting to understand why the outcome of the battle was so decisive, it is difficult to criticize much of Darius' deployment and plans. Unlike at the battle of Issus, Darius had correctly matched the terrain to the capabilities of his army. Although clearly facing a tactically adept enemy, the Persian ruler not unreasonably hoped that his vastly superior numbers could negate Alexander's prowess as a commander. Indeed, the number of troops Alexander committed to the defence of his right wing indicates that the Macedonian line was in danger of being undone and outflanked in this sector of the battlefield. With Alexander's attention drawn to the right, one wonders why Darius could not have made greater gains on the Macedonian left wing. As at Issus, the credit for this should perhaps be given to Parmenion, who once again seems to have held his ground in the face of heavy and sustained attacks. Darius' forces probably came fairly close to outflanking Alexander's line on both wings. However, despite the credit Darius may be given for these elements of his tactical plan, his futile use of the chariots reveals the limits of his competency. Forces such as these should rarely be used in such an isolated fashion. With infantry support to pin the Macedonian phalanx in place, the chariots may have made an impact on the battle. As it was, the charioteers were wasted and simply sent to their deaths.

Whilst correctly criticizing some of Darius' decisions, we must remember that some of his problems were caused, or amplified, by Alexander's tactical manoeuvres. Alexander's initial deployment was an excellent response to the disadvantages he faced at Gaugamela. This, in conjunction with his oblique advance to the right, threatened to neutralize Darius' plan and forced the Persian rulers' hand. By these actions, Alexander disrupted the balance of the Persian line, and in doing so created the gap into which the Companions attacked. The events on the Macedonian right wing suggest that even under severe pressure, Alexander's *coup d'oeil* remained intact and he was able to time the decisive stroke to perfection.

The battle of Gaugamela reveals in stark detail the relationship between physical and moral forces in warfare. Despite being outnumbered and thereby seriously outflanked by his enemy, Alexander's crushing physical assault on the Persian centre created a war-winning effect on the morale and cohesion of the enemy army. A penetrating attack on the opposing line creates a degree of vulnerability for the advancing forces. Rapid, thrusting attacks through the enemy's front line forces almost inevitably exposes the flanks of the advancing units to counterattacks. If such counterattacks were to occur in an organized and coherent fashion, the spearhead forces could be cut off and destroyed in detail. However, when this kind of penetrating attack works it does so because the assault dislocates the enemy's cohesion so rapidly that he is incapable of organized resistance. The sight of enemy forces in the rear tends to turn the minds of the enemy front line forces to retreat. This effect was the basis for the success of the German operational concept of Blitzkrieg. In this case, the penetration by armoured forces was so rapid that the enemy's resistance collapsed when it discovered German forces deep in its rear. Some battles are won by devastating physical destruction of the enemy, to a point at which they simply have insufficient numbers left to resist effectively. However in many battles, like Gaugamela, the enemy is defeated in his mind even though little actual destruction has taken place. Once this has occurred, and the enemy's cohesion is broken, then the physical destruction of his forces can take place during the pursuit.

Capture of the Persian Capitals

The defeat of Darius' army at Gaugamela did not signal the end of the fighting for Alexander and his men. Indeed, in the following five years Alexander would face his biggest strategic challenges, and achieve possibly his greatest battlefield victory. After Gaugamela Alexander had a number of objectives, all of which would help the Macedonian cement control in his new empire. In the first instance he wanted to capture the main capitals of the Persian Empire and establish control over its central satrapies. Not only would this bring political and organizational benefits, it would also provide substantial financial rewards because the capitals of Susa and Persepolis contained the main imperial treasuries. However, Alexander had another problem that required attention. Darius may have been defeated in the field for the second time, but he was still at large and attempting to organize further resistance. Therefore, the Macedonian king would have to hunt down his opponent to prevent him acting as a focal point for opposition to the new order.

Alexander's first task was to occupy the great city of Babylon. In the satrapy of Babylonia the Macedonians were treated as liberators, releasing the locals from the occupation of the Persians. From Babylon, Alexander marched on the capital Susa, which he reached in December 331. He was able to gain control of the capital without any resistance, and indeed was greeted by the local satrap with gifts. At Susa he gained control of the substantial treasury of the Persian ruler. In all, it amounted to the considerable sum of 40,000 talents of gold and silver bullion and 9,000 talents in gold Darics. Alexander not only captured the treasury, he also recovered Greek artefacts taken during the Persian invasions of Greece 150 years earlier. Ever the publicist, and aware of the significance of continued support for the campaigns in Greece, Alexander returned the artefacts to the Greek homeland. A further 595 km (370 miles) to the southeast of Susa was Persepolis. As the seat of Ariobarzanes, the Satrap of Persis, and the residence of the Persian monarchy, Persepolis was the very heart of the Persian Empire.

Militarily, Alexander now faced a different set of challenges. After the welcome he had received in Babylonia, the territory he was now entering would be hostile both in terms of its inhabitants and its terrain. In order to reach Persepolis, Alexander's forces would have to engage in mountainous warfare against foes well versed in such operations. The fact that Alexander was able to adapt both himself and his army to these different conditions is one of the main reasons why he deserves such praise as a military commander. Alexander had received reinforcements to replace his losses sustained at the battle of Gaugamela. However, the young Macedonian was not content with simply recreating the army that had defeated

Darius. Instead, for the challenges ahead he reorganized some of his forces to create more mobile units. New and smaller companies of the Companion cavalry were established. In essence, the ile were divided into lochi with 75-100 men in each company. In addition, 8 infantry commando units of 1,000 men were created. These new forces were specially trained and equipped for mountain warfare. As Alexander anticipated further conflict with irregular foes, the army was further reorganized and lightened in the summer of 330. To this end, Alexander trained two groups of lightly armed cavalry from Medes and Persia. One group was composed of mounted javelin men, and the other acted as mobile mounted infantry. These lighter units were complemented by other light cavalry forces made up of Thracian and Greek mercenary troops. In addition, the heavy cavalry, including the Companions, increasingly operated in smaller units in support of the light cavalry forces. Not only were these forces more mobile in terms of their equipment and tactics; in terms of command and control they became more independent. Mobility in military operations is not just about creating light forces with small logistical require-ments. Just as important as this is the creation of a command ethos that delegates responsibility and initiative to unit commanders. In modern terms this style of command is known as 'Mission Command'. Without this approach to command, unit commanders involved in mobile operations, often detached from the main forces, can become paralysed in the face of a rapidly changing situation whilst they await orders from above.

One of the first tests for Alexander's new mobile formations was his conflict with the Uxians. For almost two centuries the Persian rulers had failed to completely subdue the Uxians. Consequently, those travelling through their mountainous lands were required to pay a toll. This of course was something Alexander would not tolerate, and so by the use of military force he would compel them to accept his hegemony. Alexander's defeat of this difficult enemy relied on guile and ruthlessness. Alexander's initial response was to feign submission to Uxian demands. He agreed to pay the toll and arranged to meet the Uxian warriors in a mountain pass to pay his dues. However, whilst the Uxian fighting men were on route to the meeting place, Alexander led the Royal Bodyguards, hypaspists and 8,000 other unspecified troops on a rapid night march to attack the Uxians' villages. Having inflicted destruction on their home bases, the Macedonian force then moved swiftly to deal with the Uxian warriors in the pass. In fact, the pace of Alexander's movements was such that he was able to deploy his men in and around the pass before the enemy arrived. Whilst Alexander commanded the troops who occupied the pass, Craterus was dispatched to seize the heights that overlooked the probable line of retreat the Uxians would take if combat occurred. It soon became clear to the Uxians that Alexander held an insurmountable position in the pass. Rather than risk a suicidal assault on the Macedonian forces, the Uxians fled and sought refuge on the heights, that unbeknown to them were held by Craterus' men. In the panic and pursuit that ensued many of the Uxians died either at the hands of Alexander and Craterus' men or by simply falling to their deaths from the heights. The result of this crushing defeat was that the Uxians were forced to pay Alexander an annual tribute, and of course offer him free passage through their lands. As Fuller indicates, what is astonishing about this episode is that Alexander had defeated an enemy in twenty-four hours that the Persian Empire had failed to subdue in two centuries. The new mobile forces had passed their first test.

The brief conflict with the Uxians was a mere appetizer to the main obstacle that faced Alexander as he neared Persepolis. The most direct route to the Persian capital was via the 'Persian Gates', a narrow pass in the Zagros Mountains. However, the Gates were held by Ariobarzanes, commanding 40,000 infantry and 700 cavalry. Alexander's dilemma was twofold. He had to defeat the enemy forces, but do so in such a way that they were unable to fall back to Persepolis. Alexander was intent on seizing the Persian treasury before his enemy had the chance to remove it elsewhere. Therefore, a frontal assault on Ariobarzanes in the pass would not only risk heavy casualties, it would also afford the Persian commander the opportunity for a steady retreat back to the capital. The main road to Persepolis was not an option for Alexander's approach. This route would leave him significantly further from the capital than Ariobarzanes, and once Alexander's enemy was alerted to the Macedonian's intentions he would be able to win the race to the waiting treasure. Thus, faced once again with a challenging operational problem, Alexander relied upon his guile and the speed of his forces to outmanoeuvre the enemy.

Alexander's first task was to lighten his offensive forces still further. To achieve this, he sent Parmenion with the baggage and some of the heavier troops, such as the

Thessalian cavalry, along the main road, whilst Alexander took the Companion cavalry, Macedonian infantry, Agrianians and archers to outflank the enemy via a mountain path. Initially, all seemed to go well. Alexander's forces made good time and appeared to have outflanked the enemy. However, Ariobarzanes was prepared for such an eventuality and had arranged something of an ambush for the Macedonians. Alexander's men found themselves pinned down in a deep gorge, with their route forward blocked by a purpose-built wall defended by the enemy. Perhaps displaying a degree of impetuousness, Alexander ordered a frontal assault on the wall. However, on this occasion the well-prepared enemy, armed with catapults, threw his men back. After sustaining heavy casualties Alexander withdrew his forces and camped nearby. Alexander now had to act quickly. His fear now was that Ariobarzanes would continue to hold the Persian Gates with a minimal force, whilst dispatching the majority of his army back to the capital, in which case they could also engage Parmenion's contingent. Thus, Alexander needed another route by which to outmanoeuvre Ariobarzanes. Luckily, amongst the enemy prisoners captured in the recent action was a man who had worked as a shepherd in the local area. With the inducement of a substantial reward, the shepherd divulged information about an extremely narrow and difficult path through a densely wooded area. This path would enable the Macedonian to outflank his enemy. Despite the substantial challenges of moving troops along such a path, Alexander must have decided that it was his only real choice.

In the action to come, Alexander once again revealed

himself to be astute at the art of deception. He left
Craterus at the camp with two battalions of phalanx,
cavalry and archers. Of course, it was imperative that
Ariobarzanes did not become aware of the fact that
Alexander was manoeuvring to his rear. Should he discern
Alexander's movements, not only would he be able to
disrupt the outflanking operation, but he could also
attempt an attack on Craterus' weakened force. Here again
we see the dangers involved in the bold operations
Alexander so often used. There was always a danger that
if it went wrong, the Macedonian forces could be defeated
in detail. As Alexander set off on his precipitous
outflanking operation, he had effectively split his forces
into three sections. To distract Ariobarzanes from his real
intentions, Alexander instructed Craterus to keep a full
complement of campfires burning and to keep the enemy
on their toes. The route taken by Alexander was steep,
narrow, overgrown and approximately 17km (11 miles) in
length. Yet, the young Macedonian king proved that
neither terrain nor enemy would stand in his way. Before
the forces were finally in position for the battle, Alexander
detached even more of his men. He sent Amyntas, Philotas
and Coenus with most of the cavalry and some infantry
to bridge the river Araxes at a point between the Persian
Gates and Persepolis. Why did Alexander split his forces
even further? Fuller makes a reasonable guess that the
motivation behind this was to ensure that if the attack on
Ariobarzanes went badly, he could quickly race to
Persepolis and still capture the treasury. Bosworth, citing
Curtius, on the other hand claims that this detachment's
role was not to bridge the river, but actually to act as

148

another assault force to compound the confusion in the Persian camp once the attacks began.

Finally, after a long and difficult march Alexander's forces were in position to the rear of the enemy. Alexander's forces cleared three Persian fortifications before attacking the main enemy camp. A bugle signalled for Craterus to begin an assault on the wall in the gorge. This meant that the Persians would be assailed from two sides simultaneously. The enemy was taken completely by surprise; their cohesion was shattered and their morale broken. As they tried to escape, many of the Persians simply ran into a force of 3,000 infantrymen under the command of Ptolemy, who were guarding one of the escape routes. By all accounts, the Persians suffered enormous casualties. Although he escaped this initial assault with a contingent of his men, Ariobarzanes was eventually killed in later fighting around Persepolis. By an outstanding act of deception, and an equally remarkable manoeuvre, Alexander had inflicted a crushing defeat on an enemy who initially seemed to hold a significant advantage. To achieve this, Alexander had utilized a local source of intelligence, and was able to rely upon his subordinates to fulfil the tasks required of them.

Alexander now led the Companion cavalry in a rapid advance on the Persian capital. He needed to establish his rule rapidly before the treasury could be looted. With its substantial defending force now defeated, Persepolis was open to the new ruler of the Persian Empire. The pace of Alexander's assault on the capital ensured that he captured the contents of the treasury intact. The rewards for Alexander's success were substantial; the contents of the treasury amounted to 120,000 talents. In an act of apparent revenge for the Persian invasions of Greece, the palace of the Persian monarchy was destroyed by fire. This action would again play well amongst the Greek Community. Thus, Alexander had much to celebrate. And yet, Darius was still at large trying to organize resistance against the young conqueror. Alexander could not tolerate the existence of a genuine challenger to his power, and so the campaign was about to head further east. The great Macedonian commander was about to face his sternest military test.

5

Protracted War in the East:
Counter-insurgency and the
Battle of the Hydaspes

Alexander had entered Persepolis in January 330, and although he knew that Darius was still at large, he remained in the Persian capital until May or June. A number of explanations have been put forward to explain this delay in the pursuit of his defeated enemy. For example, it has been suggested that Alexander may have been hoping and waiting for a coronation by the Persians in a similar show of acceptance to that which he had received in Egypt. In addition, he may have been engaged in diplomatic exchanges with Darius and his entourage to put an end to the hostilities. However, the most likely explanation is simply that Alexander was waiting for the snow to clear in the passes over the Zagros Mountains. By now, Darius had reached the third and final of the Persian capitals, Ecbatana. Engels reports that because of the winter snow and ice, the route between Persepolis and Ecbatana was impassable until at least March. These harsh winter conditions in Media meant that Darius was equally stranded in his capital. Logistical demands played a significant part in the timing of the departure from Persepolis. The 827-km (514-mile) route Alexander's army would take to Ecbatana was through a region of Persis not overly endowed with fertile land. Thus, before Alexander's forces could begin the long march, they would have to wait for the harvest period and establish a series of supply depots along the route. Again, when we consider the extraordinary pace at which Alexander's army could operate, it is worth remembering the logistical demands of such operations. However, for the pursuit Alexander took with him his lighter forces. Thus, despite the challenging terrain ahead, the logistical operation was once again able to support an incredible series of marches in the final pursuit of Darius.

The Pursuit of Darius and his Successors

As Alexander reached Ecbatana, it soon became clear that Darius had fled the last of his capitals and was heading further east into Afghanistan. Increasingly, the Persian ruling elite was submitting to the hegemony of the young Macedonian. Darius was becoming an isolated figure. In light of this, the pursuit of Darius now took an unexpected turn. Alexander had left Ecbatana with the Companion cavalry; scouts; mercenary cavalry; hypaspists; phalangites; archers and Agrianians. As usual, his pace was outstanding; so much so that it is reported that horses died of exhaustion and infantrymen collapsed through their exertions. Alexander was nearing his enemy as he stopped at Rhagae (near Tehran) before he passed through the Caspian Gates. He was not long through the Gates, and on the edges of the Great Salt Desert, when news reached him that Darius had been usurped by a group of his own commanders led by Bessus, the Satrap of Bactria. However, this news did not bring the pursuit to an end. Indeed, Alexander increased his efforts to capture both Darius and his usurper. With the Companion cavalry, scouts and lightly armed infantry, Alexander pushed forward for two days until he came upon a camp recently abandoned by his prey. The Macedonian king was now frustratingly close to capturing his long-pursued enemy. Thus, he selected the 500 fittest men and rode through the night until finally he came upon the enemy at dawn. As Alexander and his men closed-in, Bessus could now only think of fleeing the oncoming Macedonian. So in order to lighten their load and affect a quicker escape, Bessus and his men killed Darius with spears and left the body for Alexander to find. Thus in July 330 Alexander finally caught up with the enemy who he had last encountered at Gaugamela the pervious October. Either as an astute political move to retain Persian acquiescence, or out of genuine respect for his royal status, Alexander gave Darius a royal burial at Persepolis.

The death of Darius and the capture of the third and final Persian capital, Ecbatana, had great significance for the nature of Alexander's campaign. These two acts signalled the end of the Greek war of vengeance on its old foe. In a sense, the campaign was now more directly about the aggrandisement of Alexander and his establishment as the

Lord of Asia. Although his personal goals had undoubtedly been a motivating factor throughout, they now came to the fore. However, Alexander could still justify further campaigning as a means to secure the eastern frontiers of the new empire. Nonetheless, at Ecbatana we witness the beginnings of a significant shift in the balance of the army. With the war of the League of Corinth over, the Greek Allied forces were now allowed to return to the homeland. Those who wished to remain were retained as mercenaries. In order to replace these fine forces, Alexander had established military training for young Asians. From the fall of Ecbatana onwards, Alexander's army continued to be based on the Macedonian core, but would be increasingly reinforced by troops from the peoples of the Persian Empire. For example, in the autumn of 330 Alexander received 300 cavalry and 2,600 infantry from Lydia. In the winter of 329-28 his army was boosted by the arrival of 1,000 cavalry and 8,000 infantrymen from Lycia and Syria. In addition, he was increasingly employing elements of the Persian cavalry elite, and from these he established the 'Cavalry Guard of Persians' to operate alongside the Companion cavalry.

The war of revenge may have ended for the League of Corinth, but Alexander now had two new objectives. In the first instance he wanted to secure his new empire by conquering and subduing the eastern provinces. In addition, Alexander could not countenance the continued existence of Bessus, who was now perceived as a pretender to the Persian throne. These two objectives drove the army further east into Bactria and Sogdiana, where Alexander would face his toughest test yet as a commander. Before we

154

cover the campaigns in Bactria and Sogdiana, it is important to relate the events that led to the execution of Parmenion, Alexander's second-in-command and a stalwart in the earlier battles of the campaigns. In October 330, Alexander became aware of a plot against his life from within his own ranks. As the details of the plot emerged, it became clear that Philotas, commander of the Companion cavalry and son of Parmenion, had been aware of the threat to Alexander, but had failed to pass on the information. Alexander refused to accept Philotas' explanation that he had thought the information too trivial to pass on to the king. Thus, Philotas was subjected to torture and a trial. Finally, after he made a full confession he was executed. As these events were unfolding, Parmenion was still at Ecbatana. Although Alexander had no direct proof of Parmenion's involvement in the plot, it would be dangerous to leave such an influential and senior figure alive after the execution of his son. Thus, Alexander sent instructions to Cleander, the mercenary commander at Ecbatana, to kill the old general. Accordingly, Parmenion was assassinated whilst reading a letter from Alexander.

The implications of this plot ran deeper than just the execution of those involved or suspected. In order to prevent any future plots centred around admired and respected generals, Alexander reorganized the command structure of the army. For example, rather than directly replace Philotas, he split command of the cavalry between two hipparchs: Cleitus the Black and Hephaestion. In essence, Alexander wanted to do away with permanent large commands like that previously held by Parmenion. To further lessen the chance of anti-Alexander allegiances forming between officers and men, the leaders and the led would come from different regional backgrounds. He was also intent on limiting the influence of those veterans from Parmenion's generation. Thus, increasingly he promoted those who owed their allegiance more to himself rather than to the spirit of his father. Indeed, the divisional commands were given to those, such as Craterus, Hephaestion, Perdiccas and Coenus, who had been involved in the trial and murder of Philotas and Parmenion. As the campaigns progressed, Alexander would become increasingly paranoid about plots to overthrow him from within his own ranks. Although that paranoia may have been largely unjustified, there was certainly increasing disquiet amongst the veteran Macedonians. Their concerns related especially to the increasing influence of Persians and their ways in the court and army. These events are significant because they reveal that military decisions, such as the nature of command within an army, are not always taken on the basis of military rationale. Other factors, such as politics and personality, can play just as important roles when decisions are being taken.

In the spring of 329 Alexander reached the Hindu Kush Mountains. He was now heading into modern day Afghanistan. As Alexander headed further towards the Bactrian capital, Bactra, it became apparent that Bessus was conducting a 'scorched-earth' policy in some areas, thereby denying Alexander easy sources of supply. As he advanced, Alexander continued with his policy of founding cities to help cement his imperial rule and act as bases of operation. With the city of Alexandria under the Caucasus established, he now led his army on the long and arduous journey through the Khawak Pass into Bactria. Ahead, Bessus had headed north with his forces over the Oxus River towards Sogdiana. However, because Bessus was abandoning Bactria he failed to muster the majority of the famous Bactrian cavalry. Without an organized defence of their territory, the Bactrians accepted Alexander's hegemony without resistance as he entered Bactra. However, this did not satisfy Alexander, who still sought to put an end to Bessus' claim to the Persian throne. Thus, the Macedonian headed north from Bactra towards the Oxus. In order to delay Alexander's pursuit, Bessus had all the riverboats along the Oxus burned. However, this was of little avail against a commander of Alexander's determination; especially as he was leading an army so versed in difficult river crossings. As they had done years earlier at the Danube, Alexander's army improvised rafts from stuffed skins and crossed the wide river. Once over the Oxus, Alexander could push northwards in pursuit of Bessus as he headed towards the river Jaxartes. However, ironically Bessus' fate would match that of Darius. With Alexander's forces rapidly closing-in, two Sogdian nobles, Spitamenes and Dataphernes, arrested Bessus. These two associates of Bessus had decided to sacrifice their increasingly isolated ally in order to win favour with Alexander. The pretender to the throne was mutilated in Bactra before being returned to Ecbatana, where he would face further punishment and ultimately execution at the hands of the Persians.

Insurgency in Bactria and Sogdiana

With Bessus finally dealt with, for the moment Alexander could enjoy his relatively easy conquest of Bactria and Sogdiana. He occupied the capital of Sogdiana, Samarkand, without opposition. From here, he marched to the Jaxartes, which represented the northern boundary of the Persian Empire. In an attempt to stabilize his control of the region he entered into treaty negotiations with the Scythians, who lived both north and south of the Jaxartes. In addition, just to the south of the great river he established another city, *Alexandria the Farthermost*. However, the relative peace and stability was short lived. Alexander's garrison forces in the region were attacked as the satrapies of Bactria and Sogdiana rose in rebellion against Macedonian rule. To make matters worse, Scythian forces began to gather in support of the rebellion. For a commander who is noted for his quick and decisive victories over Darius on the battlefield, this rebellion against his rule would prove that Alexander was also capable of conducting protracted campaigns against irregular forces in difficult terrain. For the next eighteen months Alexander slowly managed to extinguish the fire of insurrection. The leading figure behind the rebellion was Spitamenes, who had managed to attract elements of the Bactrian cavalry to his cause.

Faced with an array of enemies across a wide area of operations, Alexander had to move quickly to prevent his forces being overwhelmed by coordinated action by his foes. His first objective was to secure control of the seven fortified cities established by the Persians in the region

158

around the Jaxartes. Gaining control of these would give his forces bases of operations; would help to stabilize the frontier against the Scythians; and would enable Alexander to show his intent to others considering joining the uprising. Craterus was sent to lay siege to Cyropolis, the largest of the seven cities, whilst other cities were taken relatively quickly by additional detachments. In fact, Alexander's forces managed to capture most of the forts in just two days. The forts fell rapidly as a result of the substantial technical and tactical superiority of the Macedonian army. The cities' defences were constructed of mud-bricks, which fell easily to the siege engines and techniques of Alexander's forces. For example, at a fort named Gaza the initial assault was conducted under the cover of a missile barrage that cleared the enemy defenders from the walls. With a force of slingers, archers, javelin-men and catapults pinning down the enemy, the siege ladders could be erected quickly. Once the forts had been captured, Alexander dealt harshly with those inside. All the men of military age were killed and the women and children enslaved. This policy had objectives in mind. In the first instance, by killing the men Alexander was steadily depleting the manpower for future uprisings. In addition, such actions could have a deterrent effect on other potential rebels in the locality.

Although the fortified cities were falling quickly, the resistance was sometimes fierce. This was particularly the case at Cyropolis, and it took an innovative response from Alexander to finally capture this city. The defences of Cyropolis were far more robust than the other cities, and so a frontal assault on the walls would not bring such quick results. However, a partially dry riverbed ran through the city and provided a weak spot in the defences. So, whilst battering rams were employed against the main walls, Alexander led an elite force through the riverbed to open up the defences from within. Alexander and his force of hypaspists, Agrianians and archers were involved in fierce fighting inside the city before the walls were breached. Although ultimately successful, the assault on Cyropolis was a costly affair. Many good troops were killed in the fighting, and both Craterus and Alexander were seriously wounded. Indeed, Alexander came close to death as a result of his wounds. He was struck heavily on the head and neck from an attack with a stone. This attack left him initially unconscious, and then worryingly left him without sight and speech for a period of time. However, the outcome was much worse for the Sogdians, who lost 8,000 during the fighting and received the usual punishment from the Macedonians in the aftermath of the siege.

The fall of the seven fortified cities provided only brief respite for Alexander. News soon arrived that Spitamenes had besieged the Macedonian garrison in Samarkand. Alexander was busy preparing his move against the main Scythian forces, and so he dispatched a force of 60 Companions, 800 mercenary cavalry and 1,500 mercenary infantry to relieve his men under siege. Alexander faced two main challenges in relation to the Scythians. Firstly, he would have to get his forces across the Jaxartes in the face of Sycthian bowmen. Then, if he could create a bridgehead and establish a presence on the opposite bank, the next challenge was to bring the Scythian horsemen to battle in a concentrated fashion. The operations to achieve these goals once again reveal the superiority of a well-organized and experienced military force facing less competent foes. In order to suppress the threat from the enemy's archers on the opposing bank, Alexander had catapults deployed on boats, and thereby his forces could outshoot the Scythians. With the enemy pinned-down, Alexander's slingers and archers could establish a bridgehead and provide covering fire as the phalangites and cavalry disembarked.

The first objective had been achieved. Now the more difficult challenge had to be faced: how to bring a mobile and wily foe to battle. Alexander's answer to this conundrum was to offer the enemy some tempting bait in order to lure them into a trap. Alexander and his father had some experience of Scythian tactics in their European campaigns. The Scythian horsemen tended to conduct a series of hit-and-run attacks against enemy forces. They would do this mainly by riding in a circular fashion round the enemy whilst inflicting casualties on them with arrows. To neutralize this tactic, Alexander sent forward the Greek mercenary cavalry with four squadrons of lancers. As anticipated, the Scythians took the bait and employed their traditional tactics. From the Scythians' perspective it must have appeared that Alexander's light troops, deployed in line, were merely looking on helplessly at these events. In fact, these forces were acting as a screen for the deployment of the Companion cavalry. As the enemy continued to circle the Greek cavalry and lancers, Alexander launched the Companion cavalry in three hipparchies. One hipparchy assaulted the Scythian circle head-on, whilst the other two attacked the sides of the enemy's formation. Thus, the Scythians' tactical formation was thrown into confusion and they fled the field of battle.

161

The loss of 1,000 men, compared to Macedonian losses of 60 cavalry and 100 infantry, compelled the Scythian king to submit to Alexander's rule. Alexander had achieved another decisive victory through knowledge of his enemy, an ingenious tactical response, and forces that were adaptable and capable enough of carrying out such a manoeuvre. This again shows the relationship between the instrument and the commander. A serious deficiency in either could prove fateful. Thankfully for the Macedonians, they excelled in both elements of this equation.

With the capture of the fortified cities and the defeat of the Scythian forces massing to the north, Alexander had now pacified northern Sogdiana. However, not everything was going his way. Just as he was enjoying his victory over the Scythians, news reached him of the fate of the relief force he had sent to Samarkand. Having lifted the siege of the garrison there, the relief force had been ambushed whilst in pursuit of Spitamenes and almost wiped-out. Of the original force of over 2,300, only 40 cavalry and 300 infantry had survived. Despite the recent notable successes, rebellion against Alexander's presence continued to flare-up. As he had done during the Balkans campaign, the young Macedonian ruler had to redeploy his forces swiftly in order to deal with another rising threat. Alexander took the elite of his army, composed of half of the Companion cavalry, Agrianians, archers and commando infantry, on a rapid march to Samarkand. It is reported that the force kept up a remarkable pace and covered the 278 km (172 miles) in just over three days. As Alexander approached the besieged city, Spitamenes fled with his forces. Unable to come to grips with the enemy, Alexander set about quashing the rebellious spirit amongst the local populous. His forces were now in the well-populated western part of Sogdiana, and began devastating the area. The main fortresses were captured and their populations massacred or enslaved. As Alexander had begun to face more prolonged resistance to his rule, his campaigns were becoming more brutal and less subtle in their strategies. As the weather worsened towards the end of 329, the army was withdrawn into winter quarters at Bactra. Whilst at Bactra, Alexander received much-needed reinforcements with the arrival of 2,600 cavalry and 19,400 infantry. The majority of these troops were Greek mercenaries, but they also included cavalry and infantry from both Lycia and Syria.

Conscious of the need to prevent the spread of rebellion any further, Alexander began his operations in 328 as soon as the conditions permitted. Craterus was left with forces to garrison Bactria, whilst Alexander restarted the campaign in Sogdiana. With pockets of resistance across the satrapy, Alexander divided his army there into five mobile detachments. The king commanded one detachment, whilst Coenus and Artabazus, Hephaestion, Ptolemy and Perdiccas commanded the others. Their tasks were those of classic counter-insurgency: search and destroy missions against the rebels, with pacification of an area as the ultimate objective. What seems to have been missing from Alexander's strategy was a concerted hearts and minds policy. Throughout the summer of 328 Spitamenes continued to undermine Alexander's control of the region. He did this by engaging in hit-and-run tactics with his Massagetae allies, against Macedonian forts and forces.

To make matters worse, in the autumn of 328 a combination of Alexander's excessive drinking and paranoia led to the death of Cleitus, the commander of the Companion cavalry and the man who had saved the king's life at the Granicus. During a banquet, the two old companions got into a heated argument over the achievements of Alexander relative to his father's. During the alcohol-fuelled quarrel Alexander murdered Cleitus by running him through with a pike. Although Alexander immediately regretted his actions, indeed he tried to kill himself in the immediate aftermath, further damage had been done to the cohesion of the army. One element of effective command is the trust that exists between the commander and his subordinates. Alexander was clearly undermining that trust, especially amongst the old guard.

Despite these setbacks, over the year the tide began to turn in Alexander's favour. A number of Bactrian and Sogdian cavalrymen elected to join Alexander's ranks. It seemed that they yearned the stability that Alexander's rule offered, rather than a continuation of the conflict. In addition, the establishment of settlements and a series of hill forts had essentially sealed off Bactria from Spitamenes. The rebel leader was now confined to operating largely in Sogdiana. As the next winter approached, Alexander deployed Coenus to the north with a force of 400 Companion cavalry, mounted javelin-men, the Bactrian and Sogdian cavalry and two brigades of phalanx. Coenus was given the task of intercepting any raiding parties coming from the north. It was not long before Spitamenes presented Coenus with a golden opportunity to fulfil his mission. The rebel leader invaded Sogdiana with a force that included 3,000 of his Massagetae allies. Once again, Alexander's forces were able to bring the elusive enemy to battle, and during fierce fighting Spitamenes' forces suffered the loss of 800 cavalry before fleeing back into the desert. Spitamenes' allies were quickly losing faith in his leadership. And when they thought Alexander himself was leading a force against them they killed Spitamenes and delivered his head to the Macedonian king. Once again, Alexander's constant military pressure had forced his enemies to rid him of a troublesome opponent.

With the death of Spitamenes, the rebellion was rapidly losing any momentum it had left. However, a number of the rebels had taken refuge at the 'Sogdian Rock', a supposedly impregnable natural fortress atop a sheer rock-face. Like the Romans at Masada, Alexander wanted to make it clear to those who opposed him that they could never escape his relentless pursuit. If he could take the Sogdian Rock then the symbolism of that seemingly impossible act could extinguish the fire of rebellion once and for all. The Sogdians also made the mistake of goading Alexander by claiming that he would need 'flying men' to be able to breach the defences of their citadel. Alexander provided the next best thing, by assaulting the rock with 300 volunteers trained in mountaineering. Although thirty of their number fell to their deaths, the troops scaled the rock face at night and by dawn had unfurled flags on the summit. The Sogdians assumed a considerable force had breached their defences and surrendered. Military force does not always have to be used in large numbers to achieve its goals. A well-orchestrated raid by minimal forces can have disproportionate effects on the will of the enemy.

The fall of the Sogdian Rock left only a few remaining

rebel outposts to be dealt with. One in particular, the 'Rock of Chorienes', posed a challenge because it was surrounded by a deep ravine. This presented another opportunity to display the qualities of the Macedonian siege techniques. The ravine was bridged whilst a screen protected those working from enemy missiles. With the bridge secure, the Macedonians could begin to assault the fortress with arrow-firing catapults. Again, the psychological impact of these determined operations was such that the rebel leader, Chorienes, surrendered to Alexander. The Macedonian ruler treated Chorienes and his people leniently, and was rewarded with the promise of supplies. The final pockets of resistance were mopped-up by Craterus, and thus ended almost two years of campaigning to suppress the rebellion. Alexander cemented his relationship with the conquered peoples through a series of marriages, including his own with Roxanne, the daughter of a local ruler, Oxyartes. The region was further stabilized through the prosperity provided by the eight cities founded by Alexander, and by the absence of nomadic raids under the new ruler. Alexander left behind a garrison force of 3,500 cavalry and 10,000 infantry. However, he was able to swell his ranks with cavalry forces from the Bactrians, Sogdians, Massagetae and Dahae. It was now spring 327, and Alexander was ready to lead the army in its next big campaign, the invasion of India.

The Battle of the Hydaspes

Alexander advanced into India with the intention of finding a great ocean that would represent the natural limits of his new empire in the east. The army was divided into two sections. Alexander led the elite forces via a northern route into the Swat Valley, whilst Hephaestion took the rest of the army through the Khyber Pass and along the main road into India. The invasion was partially facilitated by early representations from various Indian rulers, such as the leader of Taxila. The political and strategic landscape of India was characterized by a series of competing kingdoms. Thus, as Alexander approached, some local rulers submitted quickly to the new power in the region so that they might gain at the expense of local rivals. However, just as often the response to Alexander's approach was resistance. The fighting resembled that in Bactria and Sogdiana, in which decentralized command and control facilitated mobile search and destroy operations. In addition, local centres of population would be taken and garrisoned to act as stabilizing bases of operation. What is also evident in these campaigns is the continuation of a more brutal form of warfare. For example, Alexander met stubborn resistance from the Assacenians at Massaga. When 7,000 mercenaries fighting in the service of the Assacenians surrendered and asked for safe passage from the city, Alexander granted this to them. However, having camped near the Macedonians, the mercenaries, along with their families, were taken by surprise and massacred at night by Alexander's men. In his earlier campaigns Alexander was certainly capable of brutal acts, such as the events at Tyre. However, in most instances such acts represented only part of a well-balanced strategic approach. Now, as the resistance to his rule had increased the further east he travelled, Alexander became much less subtle in his

167

use of terror as a coercive tool of strategy. It is fair to speculate that as Alexander became increasingly paranoid about plots to undermine him, his military strategy may have been increasingly influenced by personal feelings for revenge on those who resisted. The great military genius seems to have been increasingly motivated by emotional forces, and was thus losing his strategic touch and the loyalty of his men.

Refugees fled before Alexander's army as it marched through the Swat Valley, and sought refuge where they could. A large group of the Assacenians must have felt secure in their seemingly impregnable rock fortress of Aornos in the Indus Valley. The fortress stood atop a steep and craggy rock face over 1.5 km (1 mile) high. On the top there lay a fertile plateau with its own supply of spring water. A frontal assault was out of the question. Nevertheless, this was the sort of tactical challenge that Alexander relished and had become so adept at over the years. Again, the rationale for taking on such a challenge was most likely to demonstrate the futility of resistance in the face of Alexander's military prowess. However, there were equally powerful personal egotistical forces at work within the young king. Legend had it that Alexander's hero, Heracles, had failed to capture the fortress. Thus, *pothos* (a longing) also drove Alexander to attempt the seemingly impossible and capture the rock. With a frontal assault unlikely to succeed, Alexander again displayed an acute understanding of the indirect approach mixed with inventive and careful siege work. Again, local intelligence was crucial in identifying a winding, rocky path that would outflank the natural frontal defences of the fortress. An arduous two-day march along this path, during which the enemy had to be cleared, brought Alexander's forces to a position that overlooked the plateau across a ravine. The Macedonians had outflanked the enemy defences to a degree, but still faced the problem of crossing the ravine, which was approximately 500 m (547 yd) wide and 30 m (32 yd) deep. Whilst the enemy was pinned-down by catapults, an artificial causeway was constructed to bridge this gap. From the causeway, an audacious raid captured a peak close to the enemy. Faced with the inevitability of a Macedonian assault on the fortress, the Indians attempted to sue for peace, and then attempted to escape during the night. Alexander deliberately removed guards from one possible escape route, and thus tempted the Indians into a trap. As the enemy tried to escape they were ambushed and some were massacred. Alexander's brilliant tactical accomplishment had brought to an end the resistance of the Assacenians.

In the spring of 326 Alexander and his men joined the rest of the army at Hund on the Indus. Here, Hephaestion's engineers had already bridged the great river. Once over the Indus, Alexander met with the ruler of Taxila, King Ambi. Ambi had made earlier friendly representations to the Macedonian. However, this alliance brought Alexander into conflict with the Rajah Porus, an enemy of Ambi. Porus intended to block Alexander's route, and was massing his army on the opposite banks of the next great river, the Hydaspes. Alexander's army now numbered approximately 80,000, with a core of 15,000 Macedonians. However, at the Hydaspes he would face 35,000 Indians with only a fraction of the army available to him. And although the quality of the Indian forces was questionable, there were a range of factors against Alexander. In the first instance, he had to advance quickly to the Hydaspes before the monsoon and melting snows made the river impassable. Once he reached the river, he would have to make an opposed crossing against a competent foe with local knowledge of the terrain. The speed of his advance is again remarkable; especially if we consider that he had to disassemble the crossing boats and carry them in sections across the land on oxcarts. Once he reached the Hydaspes, Alexander could view the enemy that faced him. Porus had assembled approximately 30,000 foot soldiers, 4,000 cavalry, 300 chariots and 200 elephants. These forces occupied the riverbank at all of the main fording points in the immediate area. Alexander's task was further complicated by the fact that his horses would not cross the river in the face of the elephants; the smell of these creatures would spook the cavalry mounts. Faced with these tactical circumstances, Alexander would clearly have to engineer a situation in which he could get forces across the river unopposed. This meant deceiving Porus over the position of the initial crossing point. In order to achieve this, Alexander would have to perform something of a balancing act. Clearly, he could not hide the movement of his entire army. So, he would have to occupy the attention of Porus' forces in one place, whilst slipping a detachment across the river somewhere else. The balancing act came from the fact that the initial crossing force would have to be small enough to go unnoticed, but large enough to withstand an initial assault from the enemy before the rest of the army crossed. The first force across would also have to be

capable enough to compel Porus to concentrate a substantial element of his men against it, and thereby clear
some of the fording points along the riverbank.

With his plan in place, Alexander now set about
preparing his forces for the complex operation to come. In
essence, he split the army into two parts. Craterus
commanded the part of the army that would occupy the
attention of Porus' main force. This holding force consisted
of 8,000 infantry and 3,000 cavalry. Alexander led the
force that would make the initial crossing. Unsurprisingly,
this section of the overall force was composed of the elite
elements of the army; including the majority of the
Companion cavalry; Dahae horse-archers; hypaspists;
Agrianians; archers; javelin-men and two battalions of
phalangites. All told, this leading force comprised
6,000–10,000 foot soldiers of varying kinds and 5,000
cavalry. The redeployment of such a considerable force
required an outstanding deception campaign. A whole
range of techniques was used to achieve this deception. For
some time before the actual crossing, Alexander sent forces
all along the riverbank, whilst at the same time employing
a look-alike to stay with Craterus' force seemingly
planning a crossing at that point. The idea behind
producing a lot of movement prior to the redeployment is
simply to dull the enemy's senses to troop movements. In
fact, whilst these acts of deception were occurring,
Alexander was slowly gathering his crossing force 25 km
(15 miles) upriver from his main camp. He chose a point on
the river were there was a cape that was produced from the
cliffs of the Salt Range. Behind the cape there lay a valley
in which Alexander was able to hide his troops from the

enemy's attention. In addition, opposite this cape was a large wooded island in the river. This island would further obscure the movement of his forces.

The initial crossing took place during a thunderstorm on a May night. The noise from the adverse weather helped to conceal the movement of Alexander's forces as they made their way across the Hydaspes on their rafts and in their boats. Although a great deal of planning and preparation had gone into this complex and risky operation, there was a small intelligence failure. It had been assumed that at the crossing point the river consisted of only one channel. In fact, when the leading forces thought they had reached the opposite bank of the river, they had in fact only reached another island. So, they had another channel to cross. This caused something of a delay in the crossing, and thus Porus was alerted sooner than Alexander would have liked. Nonetheless, by dawn the leading troops were across the river. As Alexander's forces were completing their crossing, the rajah now faced the classic dilemma of deciding whether the troops crossing the river represented the main effort, or were they merely diversionary forces designed to draw his troops away from the real crossing point. Alexander had seized the initiative and placed his enemy on the horns of a dilemma.

Unsure of exactly what this initial crossing force represented, Porus dispatched his son with 2,000 cavalry and 120 large six-man chariots to drive the enemy back into the river. Unfortunately for the approaching Indians they had been dispatched too late. By the time they reached their enemy they would probably have been outnumbered. In addition, Alexander would have had some time to organize his forces to meet them. Finally, the rain-soaked ground

172

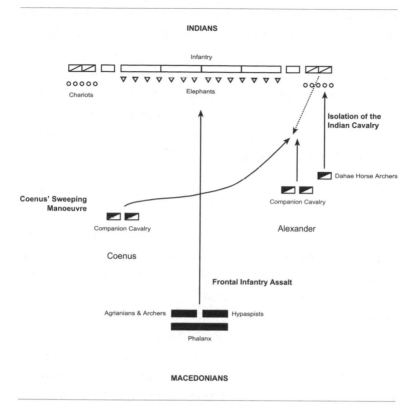

INDIANS

Infantry

Chariots

Elephants

Isolation of the
Indian Cavalry

Dahae Horse Archers

Coenus' Sweeping
Manoeuvre

Companion Cavalry

Companion Cavalry

Alexander

Coenus

Frontal Infantry Assalt

Agrianians & Archers

Hypaspists

Phalanx

MACEDONIANS

The Battle of the Hydaspes

provided very poor terrain for the chariots. The
Macedonian cavalry engaged the helpless Indians, and
routed them with losses of 400 men, including Porus' son.
It was now clear to the Indian rajah that the force
Alexander had brought across the river represented the
main effort. Porus left a small force of troops with some
elephants opposite Craterus, to prevent the latter from
assaulting the rear of his army as it engaged Alexander.
Once he found suitably firm and level ground, Porus
deployed his army in its battle formation. Covering the

173

entire front of the line were the elephants, deployed with about 15 m (50 ft) in between them. It was hoped that the elephants would deter any frontal cavalry assault by Alexander. Equally, Porus hoped that the elephants would be able to disrupt the Macedonian phalanx. Behind this front line came the infantry, who were deployed so as to cover the gaps left in between the elephants. Both flanks of the Indian army were protected by a combined force of infantry, cavalry and finally in front were the chariots.

Porus' deployment of the elephants had the desired effect, for it quickly became clear to Alexander that an attack by the Companion cavalry on any point along the Indian front was out of the question. As with the river crossing, the Macedonian horses would have been spooked by the presence of the giant and unusual beasts. However, ever the aggressive and inventive commander, Alexander hatched a plan to assault the enemy's flanks with his cavalry, whilst the various contingents of infantry would bravely engage the Indian elephants and infantry. In this context, Alexander's main concern would be to protect the flanks of the infantry from the Indian cavalry. Consequently, the first action of the battle would have the aim of neutralizing the Indian cavalry before it could emerge as a threat to the Macedonian infantry.

It is not entirely clear how much cavalry Alexander engaged Porus' men with in the initial action of the battle. If we only count those we are definitely sure were involved in the first exchanges, then it seems that Alexander faced Porus' 4,000 cavalry with 2,000 of his own Companion cavalry and 1,000 Dahae mounted archers. With such a numerical disadvantage, Alexander needed to defeat the Indian cavalry in detail. In order to achieve this he needed to pin the cavalry forces on Porus' right wing. He did this by deploying two hipparchies under the command of Coenus towards the Indian right. With these forces occupying the attention of the Indian cavalry on the right wing, Alexander led the remaining two hipparchies of the Companions and the Dahae horsemen towards the Indian left. The first contact between the two armies came when Alexander used the Dahae mounted archers to disrupt the Indian chariots on the enemy's left wing. As the enemy struggled to cope with this attack, Alexander then led the Companions in an assault on the left flank of the nearby Indian cavalry. However, this was not simply a frontal assault on the enemy. Alexander launched a series of attacks squadron by squadron. With each attack the squadrons would retreat, thus drawing the Indian cavalry away from their main line as they pursued their Macedonian prey. Once the enemy cavalry had been teased a sufficient distance from the elephants and infantrymen, Coenus launched the decisive stroke by sweeping across the battle-field to attack the Indian cavalry on the left wing in the rear. As a result of this move, the Indian cavalry was suddenly fighting enemy cavalry to the front and rear. Faced with encirclement, the Indian cavalry attempted to retreat towards their own line. At the same time Porus ordered a general shift to the left, so that the main Indian line could come to the aid of their embattled cavalry. Alexander's cavalry were now facing the onslaught of the entire Indian line.

However, Alexander's plan had yet to fully unfold. In a pre-planned operation, the phalangites, hypaspists, archers and Agrianians advanced in close formation on the left of the main Indian line. In essence, the Macedonian forces were concentrating their attack on the left side of the Indian

175

line, trapping the enemy forces in that sector of the battle-field. The crucial point of the battle had been reached, and much revolved around how the Macedonians would handle the Indian elephants. For a short while it seemed as if the great beasts might overwhelm the Macedonian forces. The elephants charged and crashed against sections of the phalanx, whilst the Macedonian horses were becoming increasingly spooked by the proximity of the great beasts. However, Alexander's men showed great discipline in standing their ground against the mighty beasts. As at Gaugamela when facing the scythed-chariots, the phalanx would open its ranks and allow a charging elephant to pass through whilst attacking the beast's flanks and mahout. Indeed, the infantry was slowly waging a war of attrition against the elephants and their mahouts. Divested of their mahouts, and assaulted by arrows, spears and pikes, the mighty beasts began to give ground and fall back upon their own forces. Confusion began to spread in the Indian ranks as the retreating elephants and cavalry compacted with their infantry troops, causing mayhem and trampling their own men underfoot. Increasingly surrounded and assaulted by the entire panoply of Alexander's combined-arms force, the Indians had run-out of options. The scene unfolding on the battlefield must have been one of terrible carnage. The Indian elephants, themselves being cut and slain by the Macedonian infantry, thrashed around causing terrible injuries to their own men. By this time the Macedonian forces were pushing forward and beginning to pursue those Indian troops who were fleeing the battlefield. The pursuit was now enhanced by the arrival of Craterus' men, who by this time had forced their way across the river.

Hydaspes: The Assessment

Alexander had achieved yet another decisive battlefield victory. And again, the key to his success had been his own tactical ingenuity in the command of a professional, well-trained combined-arms army, that could be trusted to coordinate its operations in the face of extreme danger. Again, the presentation of a hedge of long sarissae in the hands of well-disciplined phalangites had proved important in the outcome. To his credit, Porus remained in the field fighting bravely on his elephant until he was persuaded by one of his own men to accept the inevitable defeat now facing his forces. The defeat had been heavy indeed. Indian losses have been estimated at between 12,000 and 20,000 infantry and 3,000 cavalry killed. In contrast, Macedonian losses were again remarkably light with approximately 280 cavalry and 700 infantry lost. Although the battle had been an unmitigated military disaster for Porus, the political outcome was reasonably favourable for the rajah. By accepting Alexander's hegemony, Porus retained control of his kingdom and indeed had it expanded at the expense of some of his enemies.

Mutiny at the Beas and the Return Home

The Hydaspes would be Alexander's last great set-piece battle. After a month's rest, in late June the army continued its search for the ocean to the east. Many of the local tribes the army encountered submitted with little or no resistance to Alexander's rule. However, there were occasions when

177

fierce local resistance flared-up along the route. One such incident occurred at the city of Sangala. Alexander's response revealed once again the increasing brutality of the campaigns. During the siege of the city 100 of Alexander's men were killed. For their resistance the inhabitants of Sangala suffered a fate similar to those at Tyre. In all, 17,000 of the inhabitants were killed and 70,000 captured. The city itself was razed to the ground, and those in the surrounding area who did not accept Alexander's hegemony were pursued and slaughtered by the Macedonians. As a result of his alliance with Alexander, Porus gained a degree of influence in these newly-conquered territories through the establishment of garrisons.

In many respects, the campaign had continued to progress in a successful manner. However, although Alexander did not know it, the great campaign had reached its easterly limit and its culminating point of victory. As the army reached the river Beas in the Punjab, the various pressures that had been building within the army came to the surface. As the army prepared to cross the river, an intelligence report indicated that substantial enemy forces awaited them in the Ganges Valley. This worrying news came on top of the constant campaigning; seventy days of continuous monsoon rains; and increasing dissatisfaction with Alexander's own actions. On this latter point, a number of factors were prominent. Alexander's increasing use of Persian forces and the adoption of Persian culture had alienated the Macedonian core of the army. These feelings were further enhanced by actions such as the murder of Parmenion, and Alexander's claims to divinity.

So, in a remarkably courageous act of defiance, the army mutinied and refused to advance any further to the east. After four tense days of negotiations, Alexander agreed to the demands of his men, and announced that the army would return home.

The army may have been on the homeward journey, but there was still much fighting to be done. As the army headed south down the Indus River, some marching on foot whilst others travelled via the fleet, the brutal fighting continued. Alexander met resistance from the Mallians and Oxydracae. The nature of these conflicts mirrored those Alexander had fought since he had entered Bactria and Sogdiana. The cities of these new enemies had insufficient defences to cope with the Macedonian siege techniques. When the cities fell, the now standard slaughter of the men and enslavement of the women and children took place. During these campaigns one instance of Alexander's style of command stands out as worthy of attention. During the siege of Multan, a citadel where the Mallians had taken refuge, the Macedonians were making little progress. In order to spur on his forces, Alexander personally led the assault up the siege ladders. Emboldened by their commander, the hypaspists stormed up the ladder to join him in the attack. However, in their newly discovered eagerness they overloaded the ladder, which subsequently broke, leaving Alexander and three of his Companions isolated on the citadel wall. Reflecting his tactical style of command, Alexander seized the initiative and leapt into the citadel to continue the fight. The impetuousness of the king had left him in a precarious situation, surrounded by his enemies. As the Mallians surged forward to slay their

179

nemesis, Alexander was struck by an arrow that pierced his chest. The Companions around the king now bravely fought off the assailants until the hypaspists could scale the wall and rescue Alexander. The king was carried to safety whilst the army slaughtered the citadel's population in an act of revenge. Alexander's actions had certainly reinvigorated the assault on the citadel. In this respect, he had exemplified the concept of command by example. This was particularly important within the cultural context of the Greek heroic tradition. Nonetheless, Alexander had received a serious chest injury, perhaps a punctured lung, and had come close to death. Had he died at Multan, the army would have been left without its commander-in-chief in a distant, hostile land. Therefore, at the same time that we applaud his brave example, we must also question his broader judgement concerning the overall welfare of the army and the campaign.

The journey down the Indus took approximately nine months to complete. Towards the end of this stage of the journey, some of the veterans, and particularly those now unfit for active military service, were dispatched under the command of Craterus to head directly west. By late summer or early autumn 326, the main army finally reached the Arabian Sea, and could turn its attention to a return to Babylon. For the next stage of the journey Alexander split his forces into two parts. The fleet, under the command of Nearchus, would sail along the coast into the Persian Gulf and on to the mouth of the Tigris and Euphrates. Meanwhile, Alexander would lead the army along a coastal route through the Makran Desert. The intention was that the army would precede the fleet, subduing local tribes and leaving supplies along the coast for the naval forces. However, Alexander lost contact with the fleet and then faced an agonizing choice; should he march inland were water could be found, or remain on the coastal route to support the fleet. The king chose the latter course, and his army suffered as a result of the heat and scarcity of water. However, this dreadful journey through the desert provided Alexander with another opportunity to display his particular style of command. When presented with a helmet-full of precious water Alexander simply poured its contents onto the ground, declaring that he would only drink when his men could do the same. The march through the desert took a dreadful toll on the camp followers, but thankfully for Alexander both Craterus and Nearchus completed their journeys with few problems.

Alexander finally arrived at Babylon in April or May 323, almost eight years since he had left this same city. However, any thoughts that this return signalled the end of his military campaigning were wide of the mark. Alexander, now thirty-two, was preparing his fleet and army for a campaign in Arabia. Indeed, 20,000 Persian infantrymen were incorporated into the army and were to become an integral part of the phalanx formation. This was an interesting development of Alexander's army, as the Persian troops were to be armed with their own bows and spears, rather than the sarissa of the Macedonians. However, Alexander never had the chance to lead this evolved army into Arabia. In late May he began to feel feverish, and eventually on the evening of 10 June Alexander died. There has been much speculation about the cause of Alexander's death. Some suspect poisoning, whilst others indicate that Alexander may have slowly drunk himself to death. Certainly, just prior to his death, the King had engaged in some heavy bouts of drinking. The most likely explanation for Alexander's premature death is that weakened by his various injuries from battle he had contracted a fatal disease, perhaps malaria. Within this explanation, it is certainly plausible that his heavy drinking towards the end complicated the symptoms of the disease. Whatever the cause of his demise, the death of Alexander brought to an end a remarkable military career littered with success. Our task now is to explain just how such a level of continuous success could be achieved.

6

Conclusion: The Origins of Genius

By the time Alexander the Great died at the age of thirty-two, he had left an indelible mark on history. Yet the scale of Alexander's achievements appears somewhat diminished by time. It is difficult from our modern perspective to appreciate the extent of what he accomplished. However, if we take a closer look at his campaigns the results are staggering by anyone's standards. For twelve years Alexander campaigned almost continuously, and without any significant defeats. What is perhaps most impressive of all is that these campaigns were conducted against a vast array of different enemies in different terrains. This variation produced a widely diverse set of military challenges. The fact that Alexander could adapt his military technique and instrument to match these different challenges is perhaps his greatest attribute. Although he was primarily a land commander, Alexander faced an enemy that in the early stages of the campaigns enjoyed supremacy in the maritime environment. Despite this, Alexander managed to utilize his limited naval forces to great effect in support of his land campaign. Rather than try to challenge Persia for control of the sea, Alexander realized that decisive victory on land would increasingly render the Persian fleet redundant to the outcome of the war. It must also be remembered that Alexander's conquest of the Persian Empire was undertaken with an army significantly smaller than that at the disposal of Darius. In fact, the army of 40,000 men that crossed the Hellespont in 334 was outnumbered 15:1 by the manpower resources of the Persian Empire. Alexander could not simply wear down his enemy in a protracted war of attrition. Instead, he would have to rely upon quick decisive victories in the field, and rapid operational manoeuvres to maintain the initiative and momentum of the campaign. Economy of force must have been a guiding principle for Alexander. This economy of effort manifested itself in Alexander's many effective coercive actions and the non-military means he used to consolidate control of conquered territory. Thus, Alexander was not just a great military commander; at times he also displayed an astute grasp of grand strategy.

Having outlined in the previous chapters the details of Alexander's exceptional success, the book will now conclude by examining exactly how it was achieved. What were the key factors that enabled Alexander to be so successful as a military commander? Firstly, we will examine the military instrument that Alexander commanded. Confronted which such a range of military tasks, often in arduous conditions, it is difficult to under-estimate how important it was for Alexander to have a well-trained, professional core of forces at his disposal. Each of the different elements of the army will be analysed in turn to assess the different roles they played in producing such an effective instrument. Of course, the main strength of the army was the coordination of the individual parts to produce a devastatingly effective combined-arms force. However, as good as the army was, it only represented potential unless it was used effectively. Thus, it is important to explore how Alexander made use of his forces. This section will be broken down into two parts. The first of these is Alexander's command and control of the army.

Command itself is composed of a number of related disciplines. In this respect the chapter will analyse Alexander's own characteristics as a general, including his leadership qualities, as well as the process by which command functioned in the army. Just as important as command is Alexander's own tactical, operational, and strategic prowess. The commander must not only lead and manage his forces effectively; he must succeed against an intelligent foe in battle. More than that, he must conceptually and materially link these tactical engagements together into a coherent campaign, so that his military strategy serves the broader policy objectives. If this is achieved, then it can be said that the levels of strategy are in harmony. To form an accurate judgement of a commander we must look beyond his own performance and that of his forces. To this end, this chapter will also examine the quality of Alexander's opponents. As one would expect from such a lengthy and varied military adventure, Alexander faced a mixture of opponents in terms of their qualities. On occasion, opponents may have flattered Alexander's generalship. Whereas, there are other examples when the young Macedonian king was thoroughly tested. Although, on balance it is probably fair to say that Alexander never faced Hannibal's problem of countering an opponent with the quality of Scipio Africanus. Just how important this is when explaining his success, will be dealt with later.

Although generally presenting a favourable account of Alexander's military prowess, this book does not blindly attach the label of military genius to him. Indeed, Alexander's record is not one of unremitting success and brilliance. Although he was never defeated in any substantial sense, he did suffer one or two setbacks. More importantly, certain actions by Alexander produced negative strategic consequences that complicated the overall campaign. For example, the mutiny in India at the river Beas represents a failure at some level in Alexander's style of command. These flaws and mistakes in Alexander's military performance are just as enlightening as his successes.

Having explored the various factors that may help explain Alexander's achievements, the chapter will conclude by asking whether a formula for success can be identified. The study of military strategy should always seek to inform the practice of warfare. A military career as outstanding as Alexander's presents a great opportunity to help unravel the secrets of success in war.

The Instrument

When evaluating the reasons behind Alexander's success it is difficult to overestimate the significance of having a professional Macedonian core to the army. The amateur citizen soldiery of the hoplite phalanx was adequate for the quasi-ritualistic battles amongst the Greek city-states, and it could also prove effective when defending the homeland against Persian invaders. However, the limitations of this form of military organization became painfully evident when faced with the discipline and ruthless professionalism of the Macedonian forces at Chaeronea. The traditional hoplite phalanx would have proved woefully inadequate for the lengthy and varied campaigning Alexander had planned. This would be the case both psychologically, and in terms of the required military capabilities. A professional, well-trained and loyal army has a substantial advantage over less developed and organized forces. This rather obvious point is primarily due to the nature of warfare. War is a chaotic, uncertain, dangerous and physically and mentally exhausting activity. Ideally, a commander needs to know that under such circumstances his army will still be able to perform its duty, both as individuals and as a collective whole. And this is not just a case of standing one's ground in the face of the enemy. As the chaos and emotional strain of combat unfolds, a professional army is better able to maintain formation and even undertake complex tactical manoeuvres during the heat of battle. Aside from these considerations, hoplite armies were also limited because of the one-dimensional nature of their capabilities. As the previous chapters have shown,

187

Alexander's army required the flexibility to deal with regular combat against the Persian army; engage in lengthy sieges and brutal urban warfare; undertake rapid operational manoeuvres; make opposed rivers crossings; conduct search and destroy missions in rugged terrain against elusive guerrilla enemies; and scale seemingly impregnable mountain fortresses. The army that Alexander led across the Hellespont, and which he developed even further, had the training, discipline, morale and the range of capabilities required to cope with the extraordinary demands placed upon it.

When considering a combined-arms force such as that led by Alexander, it seems somewhat inappropriate to speak of a decisive arm of the army. Success in open battle was achieved by the all the elements of the force performing their roles together. Nonetheless, it is accurate to note that in most of the regular battles the Companion cavalry delivered the *coup de grace*. As a formation of heavy cavalry the Companions were ideally suited to deliver the crucial blow at the decisive point in the enemy's front. The use of the cavalry in this role was perhaps Philip II's greatest innovation in tactics. As Fuller correctly notes, a heavy cavalry unit had the mobility and speed to rapidly exploit an opportunity before the enemy could react. And because it was a heavy formation it could strike with immense power and momentum. In addition, as a mounted unit, it benefited from the psychological effect that horses could have on foot soldiers. These characteristics were amplified by the wedge formation favoured by Alexander. The wedge enabled the cavalry to shift the direction of its advance with relative ease, and was ideal for punching through gaps in enemy lines. As noted in Chapter 1, the Macedonian army had some small, but tactically very significant technological advantages. For the Companion cavalry, the xyston provided a robust weapon of greater range than the javelins preferred by their Persian rivals. Taken together, the xyston, bronze armour and mounts made the Companions particularly effective against less-well trained and lightly armed infantry formations. However, as shown at the Granicus and Pelium, the Companion cavalry was capable of more than just riding down opponents on their mounts at speed. The Companions could also engage in brutal hand-to-hand fighting as well. The Companion cavalry was a unit that shattered the cohesion of the enemy and inspired friendly forces in equal measure.

However, the battle at the Hydaspes proves the earlier point that Alexander required a range of capabilities to deal with different opponents. The use of elephants by Rajah Porus meant that the decisive blow would have to be delivered by other forces instead of the cavalry. However, even here, the cavalry played a vital role by neutralizing its Indian counterpart. This was essential to protect the flanks of the infantry, which on this occasion had the task of leading the attack. The advantages of the cavalry were plain to see in this role. In the first instance, they were able to launch a series of successive attacks to isolate the Indian cavalry. Once this had been achieved, the mobility of Coenus' two hipparchies comes into play, as they sweep across the battlefield to strike the Indian cavalry in the flank. The final attribute of the cavalry that distinguished the Macedonian art of war was the pursuit. With objectives far greater than those of the traditional Greek city-states, it was imperative that Alexander had an instrument capable of delivering decisive and final victories over his opponents. The cavalry provided this capability. The greatest slaughter of a defeated enemy was achieved in the pursuit. Overall, Philip II had created an army that, through the Companion cavalry, had become far more mobile and devastating in its battlefield performance. The speed at which it could operate and manoeuvre gave Alexander a massive advantage in terms of seizing and maintaining the initiative. Once he had this initiative, the striking power of the Companions made it difficult for the enemy to recover. Then, once the enemy's cohesion had been broken, the cavalry could exploit this further by pursuing the fleeing enemy.

The Companion cavalry has a very prominent role in the surviving accounts of Alexander's battles. In contrast there is often little detail about the role played by the other cavalry units. However, in line with the general point already made about the nature of combined-arms operations, the actions of these other units were often vital to the successful outcome of a battle. Heavy cavalry units such as the Thessalians and those supplied by Alexander's Greek Allies played an essential role by holding the left wing of the army. As noted, at the battles of Issus and Gaugamela these cavalry forces fought fierce holding actions against the onslaught of the Persian cavalry. Light cavalry units such as the Thracians performed similar functions by guarding both flanks of the army against Persian forces. Without the resistance of these units, the Companion cavalry could have been attacked in the rear as the Macedonian line was rolled-up by Persian outflanking forces.

When studying the great battles of Alexander the influence of the Companion cavalry is obvious. One can clearly identify the point at which the cavalry had the decisive impact on the flow of the battle. This is less the case with the phalangites. Nonetheless, their impact on the outcome of battles was no less great. The phalanx performed a number of functions. In regular battles, such as those at the Granicus, Issus and Gaugamela, its main function was to act as the foundation from which the cavalry could launch its attack. In this role the phalanx fulfilled two roles. In the first instance it provided a solid centre to the Macedonian line, so that the forces on the right wing could seek the decisive action without fearing that their flanks and rear would become vulnerable. In fact, the only manner in which the phalanx could become vulnerable was if its own flanks or rear could be attacked. This could normally only be achieved if the cohesion of the phalanx line was broken, or if the entire Macedonian line was outflanked. The phalanx would also pin the enemy both physically and psychologically. An enemy line facing the massed ranks of the sarissae could not risk rapid redeployment to deal with the advancing Macedonian cavalry. By doing so they would become vulnerable to attack from the phalangites.

However, the phalanx performed far more than just a pinning role. This is a significant point because F.E. Adcock claims that the phalanx did not have a striking role as such. Even in regular battles the phalanx was heavily involved in the decisive attacks led by the Companion cavalry. To illustrate the significance of this we need only analyse the fate of the Persian scythed-chariots at Gaugamela. Like the cavalry, Darius hoped that the

191

chariots would perform as a mobile striking force to break the cohesion of the enemy line. However, as noted in Chapter four, the chariots appear to have undertaken their attack in isolation from other Persian forces. Without the threat from a combined force of chariots and infantry, the Macedonian phalanx could concentrate its efforts on countering the charioteers. They did this by opening their lines and allowing the chariots to pass through. Had the Macedonians faced a combined Persian force, their freedom of action against the chariots would have been curtailed. The mistake made by Darius in the use of his chariots was replicated by Marshal Ney at the battle of Waterloo. On that occasion, Ney launched the French cavalry in a series of attacks against the Allied lines without infantry support. Again, this allowed the Allied forces to form square, and thereby neutralize the effect of this prized French asset. It seems that Alexander was conscious of such a problem. At the Granicus, Issus and Gaugamela the Companion cavalry was closely followed in the attack by the hypaspists, phalangites and units such as the Agrianians. Indeed, at the Granicus Arrian describes how the light troops joined the Companions in their attack on the Persian frontline. He describes a similar scene at Gaugamela, when the phalanx added to the weight of the Companions' attack to breach the Persian line. Of course, the most obvious example of a phalanx attack was at the Hydaspes, where the phalanx, hypaspists, Agrianians and archers undertook a frontal assault on the Indian line.

The use of the phalanx in irregular conflicts also throws into question Adcock's assertion concerning the offensive role of this formation. Against the Triballians at the wooded glen Alexander led the phalanx in a frontal assault that breached the enemy's centre. The phalangites also seem to have performed as front line assault troops in some of Alexander's sieges. For example, in the final stages of the siege at Tyre Alexander led the phalanx in a combined attack with the hypaspists on a breach in the city's wall. Against irregular, lightly armed foes the heavily armed phalanx often proved so intimidating that combat was not required. As in traditional hoplite warfare, often the mere sight of a well-disciplined phalanx was enough to coerce the enemy. This was certainly the case at Pelium, when Alexander used the phalanx in a display of battlefield drill that revealed both its discipline and immense striking power. Without any contact at all, the coercive effect of the phalanx cleared enemy forces from the surrounding hills. In the hands of Alexander, the professional and well-trained phalangites were a versatile and dependable element of his combined-arms force. They were undoubtedly crucial to the success of his campaigns. Technologically, they had an edge over the opponents they faced. Armed with the sarissa, if the Macedonian phalanx maintained its cohesion it was a formidably armed formation. However, in theory the size of the sarissa could make the phalanx somewhat cumbersome. And yet, this does not particularly seem to have been the case. The manoeuvres at Pelium, if conducted with the sarissa, suggest that the phalangites were so well trained that complex and rapid changes of direction were possible without losing cohesion. Once again, the emphasis is on the quality of the forces.

The success Alexander enjoyed against his many enemies cannot be fully understood without reference to the hypaspists. This elite unit of infantry proved to be crucial in conflict across the spectrum of warfare. It represented a well-trained, flexible and reliable force that Alexander could call upon for difficult and/or crucial operations. On the regular battlefield it played the pivotal role of linking the advancing cavalry to the infantry phalanx and the rest of the army. In this sense, the hypaspists seem to perform two functions. In the first instance they helped maintain continuous physical contact between the rapidly advancing cavalry and the slower moving units. This was crucial in preventing any significant gap appearing in the Macedonian line. In addition, because they could move at pace they were probably the first infantry force to engage the enemy behind the cavalry. This helped to prevent the danger of an isolated and unsupported cavalry assault. One can imagine a situation in which the enemy is faced with the heavy Companion cavalry, led by Alexander himself, charging at pace towards them. Following closely behind were the hypaspists, ready to complicate the tactical situation for the enemy and help exploit the imminent breach in the line. Not far behind the hypaspists comes the phalanx's wall of sarissae, ready to drive the enemy back and into further confusion. With such a vision, it is easier to appreciate why the Persian lines collapsed so rapidly once the decisive blow had been delivered. The hypaspists performed other duties on the battlefield though. At the Granicus, alongside the phalanx, they led the frontal assault on the Greek mercenaries, whilst the cavalry attacked the flanks. At Issus, they played a critical secondary role by helping to save a section of the phalanx as it came under pressure from the Greek mercenaries in the aftermath of the split in the Macedonian line. One can imagine that the pace of the hypaspists, allied to their tactical prowess, meant they could redeploy quickly and engage the Greek mercenaries first, pinning them down before the phalanx arrived.

As an elite unit Alexander could rely upon the hypaspists in a range of situations beyond the regular battlefield. As already noted, in the final stages of the siege at Tyre, the hypaspists were the first forces to launch an assault on a breach in the wall. That they were given the responsibility to lead such an attack speaks volumes about Alexander's faith in them. We gain a similar insight into the status of the hypaspists from the action at Cyropolis. Alongside the archers and Agrianians, Alexander took the elite hypaspists with him on the daring raid into the city through the dry riverbed. Finally, at the siege of Multan it was the hypaspists that eventually came to Alexander's aid, as he and three of his Companions were isolated in the citadel. The hypaspists had proved a valuable tool for Alexander throughout his campaigns, but he also owed them his life for their actions at Multan.

Amongst the other units within the army, the archers and Agrianians deserve special attention. As the campaigns progressed, both of these units became mainstays of Alexander's leading formations. Described as an elite light infantry unit, the Agrianians play critical roles protecting the flanks of the army in the major battles. However, they were far more than just a defensive unit. At the battles of Issus and Gaugamela the Agrianians were part of Alexander's offensive formation headed by the Companion cavalry. While at the Hydaspes the Agrianians joined the

195

frontal assault on the Indian line in conjunction with the phalangites, hypaspists and the archers. The latter unit is surprisingly active in many of Alexander's key engagements. This suggests a significantly more prominent role for the archers than had been the case during the traditional hoplite period. Sadly, there are few precise details regarding the tactical use made of the archers. However, what we do know is revealing. Unsurprisingly, in many instances the archers were used to suppress the enemy at range so as to cover Macedonian manoeuvres. They were used in this capacity to facilitate the crossing of the river Eordaicus during the actions around Pelium. The archers played a more directly offensive role during the crossing of the river Jaxartes. Although the threat from the Scythian archers was initially neutralized by Alexander's catapults, the lead units across the river were missile troops, including the archers. Once they were across the river, these forces pinned-down the enemy to cover the disembarkation of the phalangites and cavalry. This action shows a remarkable degree of confidence on Alexander's part in the ability of the archers and slingers to fend for themselves for a period of time.

In addition to these units, Alexander was also able to draw upon the services of a wide range of effective support forces. In this category the most obvious candidates are the siege engineers. From the descriptions of the campaigns in the previous chapters it is clear that the capture of enemy cities and fortifications was critical to the overall venture. The capture of such places usually had political, military, economic or coercive significance. Without the skill and innovation showed by Alexander's siege engineers many of these strongholds would either not have fallen, or their capture would have required a very lengthy investment. In fact, without successful sieges such as that at Tyre it is tempting to suggest that the Persian fleet may not have been neutralised. Equally, Alexander's remarkable capture of Rock Aornos would not have happened. It is interesting to note that Alexander appears to have assaulted every city that resisted him. And for the most part, perhaps with the exception of the citadel at Halicarnassus, he chose to attack them directly rather than simply invest them over a long period of time. This can perhaps be explained by the fact that Alexander did not have enough forces to be able to invest a whole raft of cities along the way. Just as importantly, he understood the coercive impact that sieges such as Tyre could have. Without his siege engineers, Alexander would have been a much less effective strategist in this respect. Some of the same instruments that were used to such good effect in the sieges also saw use as field artillery. Catapults were used in this respect at the river crossings at Pelium and the Jaxartes.

Other support forces worthy of attention are those related to the logistics effort and the intelligence system. As will be discussed later, Alexander's conquests were facilitated by a remarkable logistics system. As Engels has noted, a significant part of the intelligence effort in turn must have been related to the supply demands of the army. Before the army, with its vast supply needs, could march into an area sources of supply would have to be identified. Although very little is written in the sources about the intelligence services, we do know of those occasions, such as at the Persian Gates, when Alexander exploited local knowledge to gain military advantage.

197

As we will discover in the next section of this chapter, Alexander had some remarkable attributes as a commander. However, as the above discussion has revealed, his command decisions could be put into effect by the outstanding military force of its day. Between them, Alexander and his father had created a professional, coordinated, flexible and robust force that was suited to the extreme and varied demands placed upon it during Alexander's campaigns. The fact that it could overcome so many different enemies, often vastly outnumbered, in so many different tactical circumstances speaks volumes about the quality of Alexander's army. And, although from Ecbatana onwards the army was increasingly composed of Asian forces, it still retained its Macedonian core. Also, many of the Asian forces brought into the army were of high quality themselves. For example, this was the case with the Persian cavalry. Indeed, Persian troops became part of the Companion cavalry and the phalanx. On balance, Alexander's army was also a well-armed force. However, not too much should be made of the technological edge it enjoyed over most of its enemies. In the close-order combat of this period, the tactical prowess and morale of the forces was more important to the outcome of battles. Technology does not win wars. Even on those occasions when technology was clearly very significant, for example in the use of siege engines, breaches in the enemy's defences still had to be exploited by Alexander's men in face-to-face combat with the enemy. However good Alexander's instrument was, this outstanding army still had to be led and handled effectively. How Alexander did this is the subject of the next two sections.

The Process of Command

The study of command in an army can be broken down into two elements. The first element is the process by which command is conducted. This encompasses how command is distributed throughout the army; how the different levels of command relate to one another; and how decisions are arrived at and carried out. The second element concerns the commander's personal characteristics and attributes. More specifically, this second element concerns certain mental and intellectual qualities, such as those required to make the right decisions. A commander must also have the moral courage to withstand the pressures of command. This is a substantial challenge since war is an activity engulfed in uncertainty, whilst at the same time being an arena of life and death. Just as importantly, a commander must also possess leadership qualities. In the tactical realm one of the commander's main tasks is to get his men to perform their duties despite the fear, exhaustion and chaos induced by combat. To be able to achieve this the commander must have the trust of his men. Although good military training and education can produce competent commanders, military genius seems to require certain innate qualities in the individual.

Taken together, the process and qualities of the commander produce a culture or style of command in the army. For an army such as Alexander's, which in modern terms is relatively small, the emphasis is more on the characteristics of the commander than on the process. Nonetheless, the process of command is still important. This becomes particularly significant on those occasions

199

when the army is campaigning across a wide area, such as during the counter-insurgency campaign in Bactria and Sogdiana.

In many respects, Alexander's command process was very centralized. In the military of a modern western state the different levels of command are clearly divided. Whereas, Alexander commanded the army at all levels. Within this one individual overall political and military power came together at the grand strategic and strategic levels. He also exercised command at the operational and tactical levels. Because the sources generally seek to highlight the actions and qualities of Alexander as a commander, we do not have much information about the role played by Alexander's staff. And yet, as noted in Chapter one we know that he had the services of the Royal Bodyguards, Bodyguards and the Strategoi. It is inconceivable that a commander as successful as Alexander, over such a long period of time, would not have utilized the advice of his trusted and experienced subordinates. There is evidence in Arrian of Alexander consulting some of his officers on the plan for the battle of Gaugamela. However, before the battle of Issus the gathering of his officers is reported as being mainly an opportunity for Alexander to inspire his subordinates. Overall, one is left with the impression that Alexander was always the main decision maker. Alexander must surely have taken much advice and counsel from his staff, but the final decision rested with him.

However, even in such a relatively small army Alexander had to delegate the exercise of command down through a hierarchical structure. In this respect, Alexander had a handful of subordinates who he would delegate substantial authority to. At the battles of Granicus, Issus and Gaugamela Parmenion was trusted to command the left wing of the army with the heavy responsibility of holding that section of the battlefield, whilst Alexander led the decisive move on the right. The importance of Parmenion's role, and therefore Alexander's trust in him, cannot be overstated. If Parmenion should fail, the battle would probably have been lost quickly. With Parmenion assassinated, Alexander gave a similar level of responsibility to Craterus at the Hydaspes. On this occasion, Craterus was tasked with occupying Porus' forces whilst Alexander led his men across the river. It was not just on the battlefield that Alexander delegated such responsibility. These same commanders were also trusted to command independently at the operational level. Parmenion was given command of a substantial force for the task of capturing the Anatolian Plateau. For his part, Craterus was given independent command of a detachment against the Uxians at the Persian Gates, while Perdiccas was left to run operations at Tyre whilst Alexander conducted operations in the Antilibanus. An even more striking example of delegation was during the insurgency in Bactria and Sogdiana. The nature of the enemy's campaign and the terrain required that Alexander divide his forces into detachments with their own areas of operations and responsibility. If Alexander had kept the army and command concentrated, he would have spent his time fruitlessly chasing much smaller and more mobile enemy formations.

Overall, Alexander's process of command was a sensible reaction to the challenges posed by warfare at this time and in these circumstances. For a commander like Alexander who

201

typified the heroic tradition of leading his men into battle, delegation of command was essential. Since Alexander would be at the front, heavily engaged in hand-to-hand fighting, he was simply not in a position to be able to exercise precise tactical control of the entire army during the battle. Similarly, at the operational level there were occasions when strategic necessity demanded that he divide his army and command. However, in such circumstances the overall commander still has the most significant role to play. In the first instance, Alexander had the responsibility of choosing his trusted subordinates. This is a vital task for the commander, and a test of his command abilities. Being a good judge of character of one's subordinate generals is an important ability to have. However, the overall commander's responsibility does not end there. Whether at the operational or tactical level the subordinate officers are not given complete freedom of action. They should be given a degree of initiative, but one that operates within the broader intent of the commander. This helps ensure that a decentralized style of command remains a coordinated one. It is therefore the responsibility of the overall commander to communicate his intent clearly to his generals.

So, could Alexander's command process be described as mission command? In some respects it could. Due to the limited nature of the communications systems, we have to assume that Alexander would have to give a degree of freedom to his generals. However, there is evidence that they received fairly detailed instructions from Alexander before command was delegated. This was the case at the Hydaspes, when Alexander gave Craterus fairly specific instructions on how he should respond to Porus' actions.

202

Therefore, in some respects Alexander's battles had a pre-planned element to them. However, crucial to achieving success in Alexander's battles was timing and adapting to changing circumstances. In the uncertainty and chaos of combat, these factors of timing and adaptation would have required a significant degree of freedom for Alexander's subordinates.

The Commander

Despite the level of delegation described above, Alexander was still the dominant factor in the command of the army. Therefore, his personal characteristics and abilities were crucial to the success of the campaigns. Various military thinkers have written about the qualities required for successful command. Indeed, it was Clausewitz who coined the term 'military genius' to describe that combination of qualities that enabled an individual to excel as a commander. Amongst these qualities the most important are: the intellectual ability to process large amounts of information quickly; moral courage; determination; a balanced temperament; and an understanding of humanity. Together, these qualities produce a commander with the intangible abilities of *coup d'oeil* and leadership. When this occurs, you are left with a commander who can quickly assess the battlefield, perceive the decisive point in a battle, and then can lead his men through the trauma of combat to achieve his objective. As we will see, Alexander was unusually well endowed with many of these qualities, but he was far from being infallible.

Napoleon was said to have the ability to process large amounts of information very rapidly, make a decision, and then have the moral courage required to act decisively. Alexander's actions appear to indicate that he possessed similar abilities. Throughout his campaigns he was able to unbalance his enemies with the speed at which he could operate. Although much of the credit for this must go to the army's ability to move and act rapidly, a decision had to be made before they could do so. At the operational level this was the case in the first tests of his command in the operations against Thessaly and Athens. And, when he found himself facing a rebellion in Greece upon completion of his campaign in the Balkans, his march on Thebes was conducted so rapidly that his enemies simply could not react in time. Alexander was constantly operating inside his enemy's decision making cycle, and thereby maintaining the initiative. The finest example of this at the tactical level is the battle of Issus. The pace of Alexander's attack on the Persian line seems to have caught out the Persian archers in front of the Cardaces, as well as the four battalions of the phalanx who were left behind by the attack.

When we consider Alexander's *coup d'oeil*, the ability to perceive the decisive point, the battles of Granicus and Gaugamela are prime examples. At the Granicus, the timing and point of Alexander's attack was critical. In the event, he launched the assault just at the right time to take full advantage of the Persian shift to the left to deal with Amyntas' decoy force. At Gaugamela, Alexander withheld the main attack until the Persians had committed too many of their forces to the extreme left, and thus presented Alexander with the decisive point: a gap in their lines.

204

As a commander, Alexander displayed moral courage on a regular basis. However, the siege of Tyre perhaps displays this characteristic best of all. After the lengthy and costly siege of Halicarnassus, it took enormous moral courage and determination to complete another such action so soon. However, Alexander, with his acute strategic insight, realized the significance of taking this vitally important Phoenician naval base. Alexander's determination as a commander is also evident during the long and brutal campaigns in Bactria and Sogdiana, as well as in the capture of fortresses such as Rock Aornos. In such operations Alexander also displayed the important command function of 'maintenance of the aim'. Alexander was rarely distracted from completing his objectives. This can be seen most clearly in his decision to continue with the conquest of the coastal ports after the battle of Issus. Another commander may have been tempted to pursue Darius instead.

In the decision not to pursue Darius Alexander also displayed a degree of balanced temperament. A commander should endeavour to make decisions based upon strategic logic, rather than on an emotional basis. A great exponent of this was Elizabeth I of England. Despite the religious and ideological basis of the sixteenth-century conflict with imperial Spain, Elizabeth maintained a pragmatic approach to her strategic decisions. In contrast, Philip II of Spain allowed his religious fervour and sense of responsibility to inform his strategic policy. During the early stages of the campaigns Alexander appears to have maintained a pragmatic approach to his decision-making. This is even the case with the siege of Tyre. Although we

205

cannot completely rule out Bosworth's claim that Alexander undertook the siege for reasons of personal glory, it is more likely that the main motivation was strategic logic. However, later in the campaigns Alexander appears to have lost some of this pragmatism. The plots against his life encouraged a sense of paranoia. This happened at the same time that resistance to his rule increased amongst the populations around Afghanistan and India. Simultaneously, Alexander was drinking more heavily and had a greater sense of his own divinity. As a result, the young king may have begun making decisions on a much more emotional basis. This may partially explain the increasingly heavy-handed and brutal approach he took during his campaigns in India. Alexander's style of command had become somewhat flawed, and as a result his strategy had become less subtle. This is surprising since Alexander had already revealed that he understood the psychological element of command. This is most evident in those instances when he deliberately played upon the psychology of his opponents. The most notable instance of this was his goading of Darius before the battle of Issus.

These same problems had an inevitable impact on Alexander's leadership credentials. By the time the army mutinied at the river Beas, Alexander had clearly lost some of the trust that his forces had in him. The murders of Parmenion and Cleitus, Alexander's claims to divinity, his increasing use of Persian forces and adoption of Persian ways had slowly alienated the Macedonian core of his army. The army was simply not prepared to follow their king any further. This is in stark contrast to earlier in the campaigns when Alexander's leadership abilities created an extraordinary relationship with his forces. This connection between Alexander and his army was built upon a number of factors. The fact that Alexander led by example and shared the dangers of his men was critical in this respect. Alexander fulfilled the heroic tradition almost to extremes. He mainly did this of course by leading the troops in battle bedecked in his royal armour. Perhaps the finest example of this was Alexander's near fatal intervention at Multan. Even this late in the campaigns Alexander still acted as an inspiration to his men by leading from the front. Although it is worth considering that Alexander's actions at Multan may have been partially a response to the mutiny at the Beas. In this sense, he may have felt especially compelled to act the part of the heroic leader. There is perhaps some justice in the argument that Alexander was reckless with his own life on occasions. As the commander of the campaigns it was perhaps remiss of him to risk his own life so readily. However, within the circumstances and culture of that period, it is doubtful that Alexander could have realistically taken any other approach. His willingness to share the risks and hardships of his men may explain why they stayed loyal to his cause for so long.

The sacrifices at the Hellespont and the visit to Troy to honour Greek heroes of the past had set the scene for the campaigns in Persia. Again, this reveals Alexander's astute understanding of how to bond the men to both himself and his campaigns. Displaying concern for the welfare and needs of the troops, as well as recognizing their efforts, further enhanced this bond. Giving compassionate leave to the newly married troops after Halicarnassus; visiting the wounded after the battle of Granicus; and reciting his officers' names in the line before the battle of Issus, are just a few examples of Alexander's attention to the men under his command. Undoubtedly, there were flaws in Alexander's style of command, and they became more prominent later on in the campaigns. Nonetheless, Alexander had clearly managed to marry his own abilities with a process of command that suited the challenges that he and his men faced.

Tactics, Operational Art and Strategy

So, Alexander was an outstanding commander in control of an excellent army. And yet this still does not fully explain his staggering achievements. To be so successful for such a long period of time Alexander had to have an astute grasp of tactics, operational art and the practice of strategy. Without these attributes he may have been able to win a few battlefield victories, but he certainly would not have remained undefeated against such a range of enemies. The following section will examine Alexander's performance at each of the levels of strategy, in particularly focussing on how well he harmonized his activities across them.

Tactical defeat does not always lead to failure at the higher levels of strategy. Given enough time and resources an army defeated on the battlefield can recover from such a setback and achieve its strategic objectives. Indeed, sometimes defeat at the tactical level can have little negative impact on the outcome of a war. This was certainly the case for the communist forces of North Vietnam in relation to their Tet Offensive of 1968. This campaign involved a series of operations by the insurgent forces of the Viet Cong across South Vietnam. At the tactical level, after some initial successes, the Tet Offensive was a military disaster for the insurgents. Indeed, during the offensive the Viet Cong took such heavy casualties that it was all but destroyed as a fighting force. However, this tactical defeat had significant positive strategic results for the communist cause in Vietnam. The fact that the Viet Cong were able to launch such widespread operations across the country fatally undermined the support for the war in the United States.

However, despite examples such as the Tet Offensive, in most instances tactical performance really matters. Defeat on the battlefield can have war-losing implications. It has been said that during the First World War Admiral Sir John Jellicoe, commander of the Royal Navy's Grand Fleet, was the only man who could lose the war in an afternoon. If the British fleet were lost in battle the war effort in northern France would have quickly become unsustainable. Alexander's campaigns rested on similarly shaky foundations, especially during the early years. Although his plans were able to withstand small setbacks such as that at Halicarnassus, with the limited forces at his disposal Alexander could ill-afford significant losses on the battlefield. A defeat would also undermine his reputation and the perception amongst the local populations that he was the growing hegemonic power in the region. Consequently, it is fair to say that during each of the three great battles against Darius' forces Alexander's entire campaign in the Persian Empire was on the line. Therefore, Alexander's tactical prowess was of critical importance.

Although the tactics involved in Alexander's battles were more sophisticated and evolved than those found in traditional hoplite warfare, one decisive move could still decide the outcome of the contest. As a result, *coup d'oeil* and the ability to seize the initiative were critical assets to have. Being able to identify and exploit the decisive point in a battle before the enemy could react could provide one side with a war-winning edge. This was the key to many of Alexander's battlefield successes. In general terms, his technique has been described as holding a defensive position on the left wing whilst the right wing seeks the optimum moment to penetrate the enemy line. This simplistic description captures the essence of Alexander's three great victories over the forces of the Persian Empire. However, to truly understand why Alexander was able to win such decisive victories, we must recognize that in each case he displayed brilliant tactical ingenuity. At the Granicus, having identified the weakness of the Persian deployment, Alexander's stroke of genius was Amyntas' decoy attack to stretch the Persian line. This created a decisive point in the enemy's line that Alexander exploited with excellent timing. The battle of Issus was won through a combination of pre-battle deployment, the pace of Alexander's main attack and a well-disciplined tactical manoeuvre mid-battle to save the phalanx from the Greek mercenaries. Particularly important on this occasion was Alexander's ability to bring Darius onto more favourable ground and his reinforcement of Parmenion's wing with the Thessalian cavalry. On this latter point, Alexander had recognized the decisive point in his own line and sought to strengthen it. Without the redeployment of the Thessalians,

Parmenion's men may not have been able to hold back the fierce assault by the Persian cavalry.

In many respects, Gaugamela was Alexander's greatest tactical success against Persian forces. Facing a massive deficit in numbers, Alexander's deployment of his forces gave them as much protection as possible from an outflanking manoeuvre by the Persians. However, the oblique movement of his troops to the right best illustrates Alexander's tactical prowess as he advanced on the enemy. This movement had the effect of drawing Persian forces to their left and thereby sucked Darius into committing too many troops in this section of the battlefield, and thereby produced a gap in his line. Finally, the Hydaspes is important because on this occasion Alexander proved that his tactical ingenuity could adapt to a different set of challenges. With the Indian elephants preventing the use of the Companion cavalry as the arm of decision, Alexander still managed to engineer a situation in which the enemy suffered a crushing defeat. The Hydaspes provides a number of outstanding tactical moments. In the first instance, through elaborate deception Alexander completed an unopposed river crossing in the face of the enemy, and by doing so was able to defeat some of his forces in detail. Secondly, there is the outstanding tactical action by which Alexander isolated and neutralized the Indian cavalry, thereby protecting the foot soldiers that launched the frontal assault. In addition, Alexander then manoeuvred to concentrate the enemy, and thereby ensured that the elephants would inflict maximum damage on their own troops.

As the previous chapters have illustrated, Alexander's tactical prowess was not restricted to the regular battlefield.

211

He could also inflict outstanding tactical defeats on enemies such as the Scythians, who were notoriously difficult to engage in large numbers. Alexander managed to bring them to battle with the use of the Greek mercenary cavalry acting as bait. This was followed by another brilliant act of deception that enabled the Companion cavalry to fall upon the Scythians from a number of different directions. The battle against the Scythian horsemen leads us to another of Alexander's tactical specialities: crossing a river in the face of the enemy. Prime examples of this are Alexander's crossings of the Danube, Hydaspes and Jaxartes. The first two of these examples reveal Alexander's prowess at the art of deception. At the Jaxartes, Alexander used a similar technique to that he had used to cross the river Eordaicus near Pelium. On these two occasions because deception was not possible, Alexander utilized his field artillery and missile troops to pin-down enemy forces whilst the crossing was made and a bridgehead established.

Pelium is also revealing because it shows that Alexander was a commander capable of conducting a tactical withdrawal against an enemy holding the high ground in difficult terrain. He did this through a series of manoeuvres, feints and attacks. That he achieved this withdrawal without any losses is testament to his brilliance. Finally, Alexander's tactical repertoire also included the ability to conduct rapid outflanking manoeuvres in difficult terrain. At the Persian Gates, having failed with a frontal assault, Alexander took the gamble of dividing his forces, hoping to deceive the Persian commander Ariobarzanes, and outflanked his enemy via an overgrown narrow path. With this manoeuvre he fell upon the Ariobarzanes' rear. What this episode reveals is a commander who has an agile tactical mind. Faced with a seemingly insurmountable problem, Alexander was almost always prepared to take a risk, and could engineer a surprising solution.

The action at the Persian Gates does however reveal that as a tactician Alexander was not infallible. The initial frontal attack against well-prepared enemy positions cost Alexander some heavy casualties. We have also seen how at both Issus and Gaugamela Alexander's rapid assaults caused a gap to appear in the all-important phalanx. However, even in these instances of tactical oversight Alexander's overall tactical performance rectified the situation. At both Issus and Gaugamela the same momentum in the attack that had caused the break in the line also helped save the situation. This must have been a frustrating reality for Darius. Just as the opportunity he was waiting for appeared, Alexander's attack destroyed the cohesion of the Persian line. Of course, at the battle of Issus Alexander had to take the additional measure of wheeling some of his offensive forces around to save the phalanx from the Greek mercenaries.

The Chinese military theorist Sun Tzu, writing not long before the time of Alexander, placed great emphasis on the need for speed and deception in war. Alexander exemplified how these two attributes should be put into practice. As a tactician Alexander was insightful and inventive. However, he was also a risk-taker and offensively-minded. His ingenious acts of deception and manoeuvre unbalanced his enemies. Once this was achieved, the battle was won with his well timed, ideally placed, rapid and relentless attacks. With Alexander leading the Companion cavalry at the front, these attacks broke the will and cohesion of the enemy line.

Military strategy is all about results. Being a great tactician is meaningless if your forces get mauled on the battlefield. The ultimate indication of Alexander's brilliance is the fact that he inflicted crushing defeats on a series of enemies whilst taking remarkably light casualties himself.

Even outstanding tactical engagements have very little value if they do not serve the overall strategic objectives. Ensuring that tactical actions do serve a higher purpose is the realm of operational art. As noted earlier, there are two elements to the operational level. From the conceptual perspective, for the most part Alexander displayed an astute understanding of the significance of his tactical engagements. However, to produce significant results the commander must be able to manoeuvre effectively in the theatre of operations relative to both the enemy and the objectives sought. In general, Alexander was again outstanding in this respect. The successes that he enjoyed in this area were facilitated by a remarkable logistics system. However, as in the tactical realm, Alexander was not infallible at the operational level.

A key concept at the operational level is the identification and targeting of the enemy's centre of gravity. This military term simply refers to that capability or asset upon which the enemy's resistance depends. Centres of gravity differ depending on the enemy in question. However, the most common ones are: the armed forces; commanders; cities; and the will to resist. As these few examples show, some centres of gravity exist in a physical sense, whereas some are more intangible and may be within the minds of the enemy. However, the latter still have to be got at through the use of physical forces, sometimes in combination with other

214

instruments of grand strategy. Of course identifying an enemy centre of gravity is one thing, actually getting at it may be another thing entirely. With his own intellectual capabilities and the Macedonian army at his disposal, Alexander was well positioned to target centres of gravity.

Alexander's first challenge as a commander in the Greek and Balkan campaigns revealed both his strengths and weaknesses at the operational level. Faced with challenges in both of these areas, Alexander manoeuvred his army at remarkable speed. Having out-thought the Thessalians at the Tempe Pass, Alexander arrived at Thebes at such a pace that the Athenians submitted without a fight. The ability to cover large distances so rapidly gave Alexander a substantial operational advantage. As noted by Engels in his excellent study of Alexander's logistics system, Philip had created an army much lighter in terms of what it took with it on campaign. In particular, wagons and wives were forbidden, and the amount of servants was severely reduced. In contrast to their Greek and Persian counterparts, Macedonian soldiers carried their entire panoply and some supplies themselves. From a logistics perspective, Philip had created an ideal operational instrument.

During the Balkans campaign, a force of Triballians outmanoeuvred Alexander and fell upon his rear. However, this failure in operational art was rectified by a countermove by Alexander that caught the Triballians by surprise at the wooded glen. Thus, Alexander's success at the operational level was not simply the result of speed. He also possessed the ability to assess the situation in the theatre of operations, and then undertake ingenious manoeuvres relative to the enemy. Alexander's operational art during this campaign can be

215

characterized as being a series of rapid offensive manoeuvres to engage his enemies' centres of gravity. We see this after his defeat of King Syrmus at the Danube, when Alexander had to quickly manoeuvre to counter the threat posed by Cleitus and Glaucias at Pelium. Initially, Alexander was again surprised by the manoeuvres of his enemy, which left the Macedonian having to withdraw in the face of his opponents. Yet, having made the tactical withdrawal, Alexander was again able to display his ability to surprise his opponents through an offensive manoeuvre. Having just neutralized this threat, the army had to perform another remarkable operational manoeuvre and march 480 km (300 miles) to deal with another rebellion in Greece. The pace of the advance left Thebes isolated from its potential allies. By identifying the enemy centre of gravity, whether it was their armies, cities, allies or crops, Alexander was able to make his manoeuvres count by falling upon the decisive point in the campaign.

An operational level perspective on Alexander's great battles also reveals his conceptual grasp of the relationship between tactical engagements and strategic goals. Tactical victory at the Granicus produced a number of important outcomes for Alexander. It provided him with the operational freedom to find supplies, as well as giving him the opportunity to liberate the Greek cities under Persian control. In this sense, Alexander understood that the Persian forces represented a centre of gravity. Defeating them not only gave him freedom to pursue his goals, it also helped to undermine the concept of Persian power in the minds of the occupied populations. This was also to be an important outcome at the battle of Issus. However, Issus provides us with another example of Alexander being caught out by the enemy manoeuvring onto his lines of communication. In this instance, Alexander's operational position was saved by his tactical brilliance. However, the period immediately after this first victory over Darius displays another important attribute of Alexander's operational art: the ability to maintain operational focus. As previously noted, for Alexander it must have been tempting to abandon his campaign on the coast, and instead pursue Darius. Despite such a tempting prize, Alexander maintained his focus on capturing the coastal ports and thereby neutralized the threat posed by the Persian navy. In this sense, Alexander ideally demonstrated the value of linking together these tactical actions along the coast to achieve a greater goal.

The Gaugamela campaign is less impressive from an operational perspective. Admittedly, Alexander's manoeuvres were partially influenced by the need to supply the army. Nonetheless, the Macedonian ruler's campaign in this region leaves him fighting an enemy vastly superior in numbers on prepared ground. An important element of operational art is to ensure that tactical engagements are fought only when desired and on favourable terms. Again, as at Issus, Alexander's tactical prowess saves him from defeat. Nonetheless, the defeat of the Persian Grand Army in this final battle did lead to the collapse of Darius' rule at the grand strategic level. And in this sense the battle can be said to have achieved its goal. This may have been because the army, as a physical representation of Darius' rule, was a centre of gravity. Beyond Gaugamela, Alexander's operational manoeuvres to capture the Persian capitals of Susa, Persepolis and Ecbatana again reveal Alexander linking together tactical actions to produce strategic results. These

217

events had significance both within the Persian Empire, but also back in Greece, where they were perceived as completing the war of vengeance.

After the defeat of the Persian army and the capture of the empire's capitals, Alexander understood that Darius, and his successor Bessus, represented centres of gravity in the campaigns. Destroying opposing centres of political power would cement Alexander's position as Hegemon. This part of the campaign brings us to consider the insurgencies in Bactria and Sogdiana. Can we identify operational art in such circumstances? The answer is clearly yes, although at first it may be less obvious than Alexander's great manoeuvres in his earlier campaigns. Alexander seems to have identified two centres of gravity in this case. On the one hand, there were the insurgent forces themselves. In addition, Alexander also focussed on the centres of population in the area. The great insurgent commander Mao Tse-Tung described local populations as the sea, within which the fishes of the guerrilla forces would swim. Without the backing or acquiescence of the population, the insurgency would fail. By capturing centres of population and sometimes brutalizing them, Alexander hoped to detach the population from the insurgency, either physically or through deterrence.

For the experienced siege techniques of the Macedonians, the capture of population centres presented few significant problems. In contrast, the elusive insurgent forces would prove more troublesome. However, as we have seen, Alexander prepared for this operational challenge by lightening his forces; employing and training special units to operate in difficult terrain; and dividing his army into smaller detachments for search and destroy missions. In such circumstances, operational art takes the form of a series of small engagements over a protracted period to wear down both the numbers and will of the enemy. This is exactly the manner by which Alexander brought about the downfall of the rebel leader Spitamenes. Alexander's relentless campaigning destroyed the confidence Spitamenes' allies had once had in him. Despite the odd setback, such as the loss of the relief force sent to Samarkand, Alexander had again proved that he and his forces could operate successfully across the spectrum of warfare. When we shift our attention to India, it is more difficult to identify Alexander's operational art. This is mainly due to the fact that Alexander had lost some of his strategic focus. Aside from searching for an ocean frontier, the campaign did not appear to have clear and definable objectives. Without clear strategic objectives, operational art had no hook to hang on.

The strategic level is concerned with the general use of military force towards the attainment of policy objectives. The variety and nature of policy objectives ensures that strategy is not just about the brute application of force to defeat the enemy army or capture his cities. Grand strategy usually calls for a more subtle and varied use of the military instrument. Military force can be used to coerce, deter, defend, as well as destroy. In many instances it is not necessary to physically destroy an opponent, you can achieve your ends by coercing or deterring him. To coerce requires the use or non-use of force to compel an enemy to behave in a manner in which he would otherwise not act. The use of force to deter is very similar; the difference being simply that the enemy is deterred from going through with an action that otherwise he would have fulfilled. In both instances the main target of the action is the mind of the opposing commander or decision maker. The effect is achieved by the threat to either punish the enemy, or to deny him the ability to succeed in his actions. Clever strategy was essential for Alexander with his relatively small invasion force. With the forces at his disposal, Alexander could not hope to defeat, conquer and garrison the many enemies and territories he would encounter. Nonetheless, Alexander also understood that on occasion decisive military defeat had to be inflicted on the enemy. Thus, in Alexander we witness an astute strategist, who in the early stages of his campaigns understood well what military force could, and could not, do for him. However, in India Alexander's strategy becomes far less nuanced and less effective.

Alexander was an expert at the use of force to coerce and deter. Either as a result of military manoeuvres or his previous actions, Alexander often did not have to fight the enemy. A classic example of this is his defeat of the Getae at the Danube. The manner and the decisiveness by which he defeated this foe and destroyed their city compelled many of the surrounding enemies, including King Syrmus, to submit to Alexander's rule. By this action, Alexander had saved his forces from the difficult task of taking the Triballian forces on the island of Peuce in the middle of the Danube. In this instance, Alexander had clearly displayed both his capabilities and the response those who resisted him could expect. The siege of Tyre perhaps represents the most controversial example of Alexander's use of force to coerce and deter. As noted in Chapter three, some historians claim that Tyre was an unnecessary act of brutality. Alternatively, it can be viewed as an astute strategic act that utilized military force to directly control a key port, and at the same time influence the minds of future opponents. Although there is no direct evidence that the actions at Tyre had a significant deterrent effect, we do know that the only real resistance Alexander faced after Tyre on his march to Egypt was at Gaza. Even before the siege of Gaza, Mazaces, the Satrap of Egypt, had already contacted Alexander to offer him a peaceful conquest of the satrapy.

Alexander also recognized the value of capturing seemingly impregnable fortresses, such as the Sogdian Rock and Rock Aornos. Although his actions in these instances may have been partially motivated by pothos to surpass the achievements of Heracles, who it is said had failed on two occasions to capture the latter objective, strategy must have been the guiding principle. By capturing such fortresses Alexander showed that neither nature nor the enemy could stand in his way. In addition, it was a clear message to future enemies that there would be no safe hiding places for those who resisted. Indeed, the capture of Rock Aornos was a key event that finally persuaded the Assaceni to end their resistance to Alexander.

Strategy is sometimes about the non-use of force. On occasion more can be gained from withholding force than from using it. Alexander's campaigns in Greece revealed that, at least sometimes, he understood this point of strategy. Having just gained the deterrence value from sacking Thebes, Alexander realized that Athens needed different treatment. By respecting this cultural icon of the Greek civilization Alexander showed that he could be a benevolent hegemon, and that he was acting partially on behalf of the Greek world. In his work, Sun Tzu notes that

221

often more can be gained from incorporating an enemy's resources rather than simply destroying them. By his treatment of Athens Alexander gained the use of the respected Athenian navy. As Alexander progressed through the Persian Empire, he increasingly adopted this approach and incorporated the forces of his conquered foes into his army. This had both military and political benefits.

Despite the example of Athens, Alexander's strategy was mainly based upon the offensive use of force to achieve decisive victory. Alexander's acts of benevolence could only be effective once his military supremacy had been recognized. Above all else, Alexander's hegemony was built upon the foundation of respect for his military power. With such a relatively small force at his disposal, Alexander had to take risks to seek out his foes in a decisive clash of arms. An insurgent force can afford to wage protracted campaigns of hit-and-run tactics. Alternatively, a large invading force can gain control from protracted and extensive garrison operations. For a conqueror like Alexander, his authority had to be established quickly and overtly. Alexander's three great victories over the Persian army undermined Persian authority whilst enhancing his own. At the same time, these victories also neutralized forces that could pose a genuine military threat to Alexander's conquered territories. Where Alexander succeeded in this respect, Hannibal, another famous invader, failed. Hannibal's failure was partly due to the actions of his enemy: the Roman Republic. Having been severely defeated at the battles of Cannae and Lake Trasimene, the Republic was saved by its general Fabius Maximus, who adopted the now famous 'Fabian strategy'. By this strategic approach, the Romans simply refused to take the field against Hannibal.

222

Because of this, Hannibal's conquests were never secure, and the Roman army recaptured city after city in the wake of Hannibal's march through Italy. For Alexander, the defeat of the Persian army allowed him freedom at the grand strategic level, and also gave him the opportunity to capture centres of gravity such as the Persian capitals and Darius himself.

In terms of harmonizing his performance across the levels of strategy Alexander was not infallible throughout his campaigns. However, he was proficient enough at this task to enjoy staggering levels of success. Tactically, Alexander was very effective. Indeed, on occasion his tactical prowess rectified mistakes at the higher levels of strategy. At the operational level Alexander appeared to understand the conceptual requirement to link tactical actions together into an effective campaign. Having grasped the conceptual element of this, Alexander had the instrument of force to turn the concepts into reality. Finally, Alexander performed very effectively at the strategic level. This was particularly evident earlier on in the campaigns, when his use of force both enabled and complemented his grand strategy. However, as both his paranoia and resistance to his rule grew the further east he conquered, his astute strategic performance degenerated into a less subtle, more brutal campaign without real focus. Nonetheless, we should recognize Alexander's proficiency and learn from it. In this respect, there is perhaps no better example than Alexander's victory over Porus at the Hydaspes. This is an example of perfect grand strategy, when the levels merge and the policy objectives are achieved. Alexander's operational manoeuvres had brought him to the Hydaspes with enough time to attempt a crossing before the monsoon season made such an attempt impossible. Once there, his tactical deception and subsequent decisive defeat of the enemy left Porus militarily impotent. Alexander's defeat of Porus had been so decisive that this one tactical action had produced strategic victory. Alexander then made effective use of the freedom that this victory had given him. By treating Porus in a benevolent fashion Alexander gained him as an ally, and in fact used Porus as an instrument to help cement his rule in the region.

Alexander's Enemies

To fully understand and judge Alexander's abilities, we must assess the quality of his opponents. There is a degree of disingenuousness about this exercise, because a commander can only defeat the foes in front of him. Nonetheless, for our purposes it will give us a more rounded evaluation of Alexander's prowess. On the whole, it is fair to say that Alexander never faced an outstanding military strategist, nor did his army have to engage forces of equal calibre. The Balkans campaign presented Alexander with enemies who lacked both sophistication in their military technique and a robust will to resist. In these circumstances, Alexander's outstanding operational manoeuvres and his tactical ingenuity quickly unbalanced his foes and broke their will. The Persian Empire represented a much tougher test for the young Macedonian ruler. On land, and at sea, the Persians had the numerical superiority to cause Alexander untold problems. Qualitatively, the Persian navy also held the advantage. Had these forces been under the control of a competent strategist, Alexander's invasion could well have ended in disaster. As it was, Persian strategy was unimaginative. The empire was gambled on three great land battles, and the maritime forces were never fully exploited. The Persian attack on Greece in 333 gives an indication of what could have been achieved had they enacted, and sustained, a more aggressive maritime strategy. Alternatively, the Persian navy could have been used to much greater effect to disrupt Alexander's own maritime operations in support of his land forces. Responsibility for this failure appears to lay with both Memnon and Darius. The former missed an opportunity to invade Greece when he took the decision to hold Halicarnassus. Whereas Darius can be accused of strategic schizophrenia when he recalled a large part of Memnon's invasion force in 333. Alexander's sternest test in the western regions of the empire came at Tyre, where his opponents proved themselves to be very able at adapting to Macedonian siege techniques. However, an overview of the Persian war effort suggests that the substantial resources of the empire were wasted due to the lack of a coordinated strategy.

At the tactical level, Darius was a competent, if unspectacular, commander. His battle plans for Issus and Gaugamela were logical, but fundamentally insufficient to deal with an opponent of Alexander's skill. Nonetheless, on both occasions Darius did make rudimentary mistakes. At the battle of Issus his main mistake was to fight on ground favourable to Alexander. At Gaugamela, the wasteful use of the chariots is indicative of Darius' limited tactical insight. However, in each of the three great battles the Persian commanders had a fatal disadvantage: the inferiority of their infantry. Without a solid infantry basis to their line, the

225

Persian army was vulnerable in some sense to Alexander's penetrating attacks. Although the misuse of the Greek mercenaries at the Granicus indicates that the Persian commanders did not make effective use of the good forces that they did have.

As Alexander headed further east, he encountered his most competent enemies during the insurgency in Bactria and Sogdiana. By adopting a form of guerrilla warfare, insurgent leaders such as Spitamenes managed to utilize the terrain of the area to neutralize much of Alexander's tactical prowess. This use of hit-and-run tactics delayed Alexander's final conquest of the region for almost two years. Nonetheless, over time their strategy of guerrilla warfare produced diminishing returns, mainly because Alexander's will and ability to adjust his own strategy wore them down. Also, when these enemies were brought to battle, the limits of their tactical abilities in such engagements became evident. At the river Jaxartes for example, the Scythians appeared to have fallen for a fairly straightforward ruse by Alexander. Finally, at the Hydaspes Alexander faced a commander and an army who were both incapable of dealing with the tactical ingenuity and proficiency of the Macedonian art of war. So, on the surface, Alexander's military prowess appears somewhat diminished when we consider the quality of his enemies. Yet, we must remember that in many cases Alexander did not simply have to overcome less competent foes. Often, he was fighting these enemies when they had the advantage of superior numbers and favourable terrain.

A Formula for Success?

Despite a few setbacks, as a military strategist Alexander had remained successful for a remarkable length of time. Time and again he proved himself capable of defeating a range of enemies in vastly different terrains and circumstances. This study has analysed the various elements that contributed to that success. But, what lessons can we draw from a study of Alexander's military prowess, and can we construct a formula for success based upon his greatness?

Before Alexander even took control of the Macedonian state he had one striking advantage in his favour: the Macedonian army. His father had built upon existing developments within Greek warfare, but from these origins he produced a genuinely new and effective approach to war. The force that he created was substantially more mobile than its contemporaries. This endowed Alexander with an army that on occasion could achieve strategic ends without the need to fight; the pace of its operational tempo was often enough to compel the enemy into submission. The Macedonian army also had a technological edge, which gave it a greater offensive potential against most of its enemies. However, we must be careful not to overplay the significance of this factor. Technology is a tool that only produces advantage if used effectively. A more important factor than the technological edge was the army's loyalty and professionalism. This factor provided Alexander with a force that could maintain discipline and tactical effect at times of great pressure, and also display remarkable acts of courage and prowess in times of need. Philip had also provided Alexander with the basis for a remarkably flexible army that could operate effectively in

227

many varied operational circumstances. Alexander's leadership and reforms of the army substantially developed this inherent flexibility. In the end, the army was just as effective besieging a city as it was fighting the Persian Grand Army in open warfare, or waging a protracted counter-insurgency campaign.

Finally, this outstanding military raw material was turned into a decisive and ruthless instrument through the tactical innovation of combined-arms warfare. Individually, the various units of the army were good; working together they could destroy numerically superior enemies in decisive fashion. As Philip revealed at Chaeronea with such devastating effect, he had swept away the one-dimensional, quasi-ritualistic warfare of the hoplite. He replaced it with a form of warfare that could shatter the cohesion of the enemy, before destroying them in the pursuit. The use of the heavy cavalry as the decisive arm gave the Macedonian army unrivalled striking power. However, the pressure on the enemy line was really the result of the combined-arms approach, in which the hypaspists and then the phalangites could follow the cavalry's lead. By doing away with the ritualistic element of Greek warfare, Philip and Alexander had created an army that could deliver decisive strategic effect in one afternoon. Thus, we can conclude that success requires an effective instrument.

However, an effective army is just potential, it is the commander that leads it to victory. In this respect, Alexander had an effective process through which he exercised command. Undoubtedly, the most crucial element in this was the commander-in-chief himself. However, due to the nature of battle and some of the operational circumstances encountered during the campaigns, Alexander required trusted and competent subordinates. Until his assassination, Parmenion fulfilled this role to great effect. In the chaos and uncertainty of battle, Alexander could rely upon his second-in-command to hold the left wing, sometimes in the face of fierce and sustained attack. Once the army was faced with more irregular forms of conflict, this delegation of command authority was just as important. Men such as Craterus and Coenus could be trusted to lead detachments on search and destroy missions. However, Alexander's growing distrust of his generals in the aftermath of Parmenion and Philotas's downfall changed the nature of the command process. No one general ever had quite the authority and trusted position that Parmenion had enjoyed. Positions of high command in the army were further divided to prevent close relationships developing between a commander and his men. This does not seem to have materially affected the tactical performance of the army. However, the absence of established senior generals may partly explain Alexander's increasingly poor strategic performance later on in the campaigns. Without someone like Parmenion alongside him, Alexander may have become somewhat overwhelmed with the duties of command, and/or increasingly believed his own propaganda without a senior figure to question him. The command system of the Macedonian army is not quite what we would regard as 'mission command'. Alexander appears to have given fairly specific instructions to his generals on occasion. Nonetheless, there was a degree of delegation, as required by the nature of battle and Alexander's heroic style of leadership. Thus, we can conclude that success requires a command process that suits the specific culture and character of warfare of the time.

So far, our formula for success encompasses the instrument and the process of command. And, as noted in Chapter one, the Macedonian art of war fulfils the main criteria of an RMA. However, these factors only represent the foundations upon which Alexander's outstanding success was built. Alexander himself is the dominant factor responsible for the remarkable achievements attained by the Macedonian army. This is the point at which our search for a formula becomes nonsensical. The procedures that produce a professional, well-trained army can be reproduced to some extent. However, the qualities of a military genius are intangible. In seeking to explain Alexander's success, we must look to his *coup d'oeil*; leadership qualities; intellectual abilities; and moral courage. Together, these attributes produced a commander who proved to be outstanding at all the levels of strategy, and across the entire spectrum of warfare. Alexander's ability to understand the entire scope of grand strategy; to identify the centres of gravity and decisive points; and then have the leadership required to lead his men to take these goals; these attributes simply cannot be taught. Alexander was born, and to some degree bred, to be a great military leader. When he came to power in October 336, the young Macedonian King sought to emulate his heroes from Greek history and mythology; in actuality he far surpassed even these remarkable standards. The fact that he was never defeated by a vast array of enemies, in many different terrains across the spectrum of warfare, defines Alexander as the greatest military strategist of all time.

Select Bibliography

There are many books written on the subjects of Alexander the Great, Greek warfare and military strategy. The following is just a short list of the titles that I have found most useful, and hopefully that the reader will also enjoy.

F. E. Adcock, *The Greek and Macedonian Art of War* (Berkeley, 1957).

J. K. Anderson, *Military Theory and Practice in the Age of Xenophon* (Berkeley, 1970).

Arrian, *The Campaigns of Alexander* (London, 1971).

J. E. Atkinson, *A Commentary on Q. Curtius Rufus' Historiae Alexandri Magni Books 3 & 4* (Amsterdam, 1980).

A. B. Bosworth, *Conquest and Empire: The Reign of Alexander the Great* (Cambridge, 1988).

——, *Alexander and the East: The Tragedy of Triumph* (Oxford, 1998).

C. E. Callwell, *Small Wars: A Tactical Textbook for Imperial Soldiers* (London, 1990).

Jack Cassin-Scott, *The Greek and Persian Wars 500–323 BC* (Oxford, 1977).

Carl von Clausewitz, *On War*, trans. Michael Howard and Peter Paret (London, 1993).

Eliot A. Cohen, *Supreme Command: Soldiers, Statesmen, and Leadership in Wartime* (New York, 2002).

Julian S. Corbett, *Some Principles of Maritime Strategy* (London, 1919).

H. Delbruck, *Warfare in Antiquity* (Westport, 1975).

Donald W. Engels, *Alexander the Great and the Logistics of the Macedonian Army* (Berkeley, 1978).

Arther Ferrill, *The Origins of War: From the Stone Age to Alexander the Great* (London, 1986).

J. F. C. Fuller, *The Generalship of Alexander the Great* (Ware, 1998).

Richard A. Gabriel and Donald W. Boose, Jr., *The Great Battles of Antiquity: A Strategic and Tactical Guide to the Great Battles that Shaped the Development of War* (Westport, 1994).

Colin S. Gray, *Modern Strategy* (Oxford, 1999).

——, *The Leverage of Sea Power: The Strategic Advantage of Navies in War* (New York, 1992).

Peter Green, *Alexander of Macedon 356–323 B.C.: A Historical Biography* (Berkeley, 1991).

J. R. Hamilton, *Plutarch: Alexander. A Commentary* (Oxford, 1969).

Grant T. Hammond, *The Mind of War: John Boyd and American Security* (Washington, DC, 2001).

Nicholas Hammond, *The Genius of Alexander the Great* (London, 1998).

Michael I. Handel, *Masters of War: Classical Strategic*

Thought, Second, Revised Edition (London, 1996).

Victor Davis Hanson, *The Western Way of War: Infantry Battle in Classical Greece* (Berkeley, 1989).

——, (ed.), *Hoplites: The Classical Greek Battle Experience* (London, 1993).

——, *The Wars of the Ancient Greeks: And Their Invention of Western Military Culture* (London, 1999).

Waldermar Heckel, *The Wars of Alexander the Great 336–323 BC* (Oxford, 2002).

Baron Antoine Henri de Jomini, *The Art of War* (London, 1996).

John Keegan, *The Mask of Command* (London, 1988).

Robin Lane Fox, *Alexander the Great* (Harmondsworth, 1986).

T. E. Lawrence, *Seven Pillars of Wisdom* (Ware, 1997).

Edward N. Luttwak, *Strategy: The Logic of War and Peace* (Cambridge, 1987).

Mao Tse-Tung, *Selected Military Writings of Mao Tse-Tung* (Beijing, 1963).

John Maxwell O'Brien, *Alexander the Great: The Invisible Enemy* (London, 1992).

W. K. Pritchett, *The Greek State at War*, 4 Vols (Berkeley, 1971-85).

N. Sekunda, *The Army of Alexander the Great* (Oxford, 1984).

——, *The Persian Army 560-330 BC* (Oxford, 1992).

Richard Stoneman, *Alexander the Great* (London, 1997).

Sun Tzu, The *Art of War* (translated by Samuel B. Griffith) (London, 1971).

W. W. Tarn, *Hellenistic Military and Naval Developments* (Chicago, 1930).

——, *Alexander the Great* (Cambridge, 1948).

Thucydides, *The Peloponnesian War* (translated by Rex Warner), (London, 1962).

Martin van Creveld, *Command in War* (Cambridge, 1985).

John Warry, *Warfare in the Classical World: War and the Ancient Civilisations of Greece and Rome* (London, 1998).

Josef Wiesehofer, *Ancient Persia* (London, 2001).

Michael Wood, *In the Footsteps of Alexander the Great* (London, 2001).

Ian Worthington (ed.), *Alexander the Great: A Reader* (London, 2003).

J. C. Wylie, *Military Strategy: A General Theory of Power Control* (Annapolis, 1967).

Index

sieges *(cont.)*
  Gaza 12, 119, 120–25, 221
  Halicarnassus 86–7, 93–7,
    120, 125, 197, 205, 207,
    225
  Multan 179–80, 195, 207
  Mytilene 98–9
  Rock of Chorienes 166
  Sogdian Rock 165, 221
  Tyre 11–12, 86, 109–17,
    119, 125, 195, 197, 201,
    204, 205–6, 220, 225
slavery/enslavement 57, 68,
  80–1, 116, 123, 159,
  163, 179
Sochoi 100
Sogdian Rock, siege and fall
  of 165, 221
Sogdiana 1, 12, 145–5, 157,
  162, 179, 200, 201, 205,
  218, 226
Soviet Union 19
Sparta 29, 32, 38, 50, 55
Spartan(s) 29–30
  army 38
  hoplites 30
  tactics 29–30
Spitamenes (Sogdian noble
  and rebel) 157, 158, 160,
  162, 163, 164, 165,
  219, 226
  arrests Bessus 157
  assassination of 165
  besieges Macedonian
    garrison in
    Samarkand 160

hit-and-run tactics 163, 226
invades Sogdiana 165
pursuit of 162
Spithridates, Satrap of Lydia
  80, 81
strategy 225–6 *see also*
  Alexander's genius
  grand 5–6, 219
  military strategy 6–9, 186
  Roman 121, 222–3
  Strategic Studies xi,
    3–4, 11
Sun Tzu 213, 221–2, 233
Susa 142, 217
Swat Valley 167, 168
Syria 107, 127
Syrmus (King of Triballians)
  57, 58, 61, 216, 220

Tarn, W.W. 42, 233
Taulantii/Taulantians 64,
  66–7
Tempe Pass 54, 215
Theban forces 50, 51
Theban Sacred Band 51
Thebes 50, 55, 67, 68, 204,
  215, 216
  destruction of 68
  massacre and enslavement
    of citizens 68
Themistocles (Athenian
  commander) 35
Thessalian(s) 55, 215 *see also*
  Macedonian cavalry
  units
  army 46

250